# BEARING WITNESS

## HUMANITARIAN STORIES FROM THE ARIZONA BORDERLANDS

# TABLE OF CONTENTS

# INTRODUCTION

This collection contains more than fifty stories—a small window into a vast landscape of experience. Each volunteer's account hints at countless others, especially the stories of migrants whose voices are less known, whose journeys remain largely invisible. Yet the narratives here hold threads that are shared, familiar, and deeply human. Every encounter, every moment of welcoming the stranger brings with it questions.

What happens to people we meet once they leave us, continuing toward family, hope, uncertainty? And what happens to the humanitarians themselves? How has this work reshaped their lives? How has it shaped the life of the congregation that supports them?

This book is born from questions. As long as people continue to walk through the desert seeking safety and possibility, the wondering continues. So does the call to bear witness.

# PROLOGUE

# The Beginnings of the Southern Arizona Humanitarian Movement

*by Randy Mayer*

Sometimes we look back over events and see that there was a lot more happening there than we could have ever imagined when we were actually living, breathing and walking it at the time. The birth of the humanitarian movement in Southern Arizona has had a hallowed presence that was not always recognized at the time but is palpable when you look back.

It started on Pentecost Sunday 2000, when people of faith and conscience gathered at the Friends Meeting House in Tucson, to have a conversation about the immigration flow that was being pushed in our direction. Word of the meeting had spread quietly and efficiently to people and places that had shown interest and concern for the issues that were quickly becoming an epidemic. I had gotten the word and had invited the UCC pastor in Nogales to come along.

In hindsight it was a lot like that gathering of folks in the ancient near east when they gathered on that first Pentecost. They huddled in a room afraid of the forces on the outside that were pushing in. They still had no clear purpose or mission. Some were on the edge of giving up, ready to fold, and give in to the forces of the culture.

We too gathered in a room, not quite sure what our purpose was or what we should do. Some were even ready to give into the forces that said let the government handle the problem. After all, we knew that the Border Patrol's Operation Gate Keeper in San Diego and Operation Hold the Line in El Paso had been effective in closing the flow of immigration in the urban areas of the U.S./Mexico Border. And now they were pushing the immigration flow through Arizona. The Border Patrol's strategy was to push the migrants to the Arizona section of the border where it was hot and rugged, with little infrastructure, and the Tohono O'odham land would work in their favor. The desert would serve as a natural deterrent; people wouldn't cross, but if they did, they could track them down or they would die.

The spirit began to move in that room as former Sanctuary leaders shared wisdom from their struggle of standing in resistance and offering hospitality in the 1980s to Central American refugees who were fleeing the U.S. backed wars in their homeland. It was as if the winds of the spirit blew and the tongues of flames melded our minds and wills together. Something got a hold of us and clarity began to take shape around some ways that we could take action. We talked about the underground railroad of the emancipation period, the big dipper, the north star. We started to channel the same spirit as we came up with ways that we could care for the migrant in our midst. Someone in the back said," We only hear the government's take on the issue. We need another perspective. " Another said "Why not put water in the desert?" Someone else chimed in, "We can use blue flags and the big dipper as our symbol like they did in the underground railroad days freeing slaves."

Leroy Cook was a patriarch of the Good Shepherd. His wife Marjorie was wheelchair bound for more than 10 years. Leroy treated her like a queen, caring for her at home long after she should have been in a care center. At the urging of his family, Leroy took Thursdays for himself where he could wander and explore the mountains and backroads in his old Chevy Blazer. Most of the roads were poorly maintained, rugged, and dusty, an intricate web that connected ranches and old mining claims. They ran east and west and north and south, and many were there before the Gadsden Purchase, backroads into Mexico. Sometimes if Leroy wasn't careful, he could veer into Mexico. In those days there was hardly a fence; more often than not in those uninhabited areas far from the human touch, there were just sparse piles of rocks or an occasional post that attempted to approximate that there was an important dividing line somewhere along there.

In those remote areas Leroy would often find sojourners coming up from Mexico and Central America. Sometimes he would give them a lift into town and enjoy the company. He had been a farmer in Nebraska, and he came from strong stock, surviving the plague in Elwood, Nebraska when most of his peers died. He liked to tell the story that he advanced two years in school during the plague because he was the only student and his sister was the teacher. There were positives from advancing so quickly, but there were also negatives. When he graduated from high school he was just 16. Leroy became a successful farmer and was well known in the area for his hard work and innovation. He was usually leading the pack trying new soil conservation methods. As a leader in the area he became the co-op manager for Farmland Industries for 10 years. It was in this role that he traveled to Latin America to work with some farming cooperatives there; he was always ready to broaden his horizons and share his knowledge and expertise.

When Leroy heard that there was a group of church people that was going to be putting water out in the desert to help thirsty migrants, he was the first to volunteer. His 88 years of life experience had taught him that reaching out to those in need was a natural part of his life. It was easy for Leroy to make the connection that many of the migrants crossing the border were peasant farmers, like the people he had worked with in Nebraska and the farm cooperatives that he had helped develop in Latin America.

While I didn't know it at the time, getting Leroy Cook involved was probably the most brilliant pastoral decision I ever made. Leroy was a patriarch of the Good Shepherd. Leroy was well loved and deeply respected; he lived his faith, he didn't preach or judge, he just lived life with grace and dignity and treated everyone as if they were important.

I remember the day clearly when we loaded up his pick-up truck with a dozen one-gallon water jugs, a brand-new plastic garbage can with a lid, a few blankets, packages of granola bars, a blue flag, and some electrical conduit, and headed down the Santa Cruz Valley, about 10 miles from the U.S./Mexico border. We got off at the first Rio Rico exit and headed east across the Santa Cruz River and followed the railroad tracks up to a place where a couple of migrant trails ran north. There were migrant belongings left behind: an empty water bottle with a Mexican label, a tee shirt hanging from a mesquite tree, a toothbrush under a sage bush and the trails were full of foot prints; we knew the trail was well used and active.

It was in that location between the railroad tracks that headed north and the dry Santa Cruz River that we set up the very first humanitarian aid station. Placing blankets and clothing, wrapped in plastic, in the garbage can along with the granola bars, we put the water bottles around the garbage can like anchors keeping it in place. Two or three media vehicles were there ready to document it all on camera and feed it back to Tucson for the 5:00 o'clock news. Leroy Cook was front and center hoisting up the flag, just like the classic photo at Iwo Jima. But this time it was a plain blue nylon flag atop a 30 foot economically constructed flagpole made of electrical conduit. The flag was azure blue, the universal symbol for water, a foreign color in the parched desert, painted from the neutral color pallet of pale greens, tans and browns. Migrants would be able to see the flag for miles and make their way to its lifesaving aid.

In 2000 the immigration conversation in the United States was fairly quiet, the terror of 911 was on the future horizon, and the record number of immigrants crossing the U.S./Mexico border was still in its silent phase. The U.S. population was preoccupied with so many other things. So when members of the Good Shepherd congregation turned on their televisions that night, they were treated to a heartwarming story of people of faith and conscience lending a hand in the brutal Sonoran desert. They saw one of their own members, front and center living out his faith, offering a cup of water in Jesus' name, loving the neighbor as oneself. Everyone was unanimous; if Leroy Cook was involved, it must be an admirable project, something we all should support.

In those early years of my ministry, I was led and mentored, even sheltered by the wise ones who knew the way. It was their deep roots and centeredness that allowed our migrant ministry at the Good Shepherd to become established like the old saguaro that puts down a deep tap root and then develops an intricate root system that radiates out like a web as wide as it is tall, anchoring itself on rocks to withstand the wind and elements.

# MAP

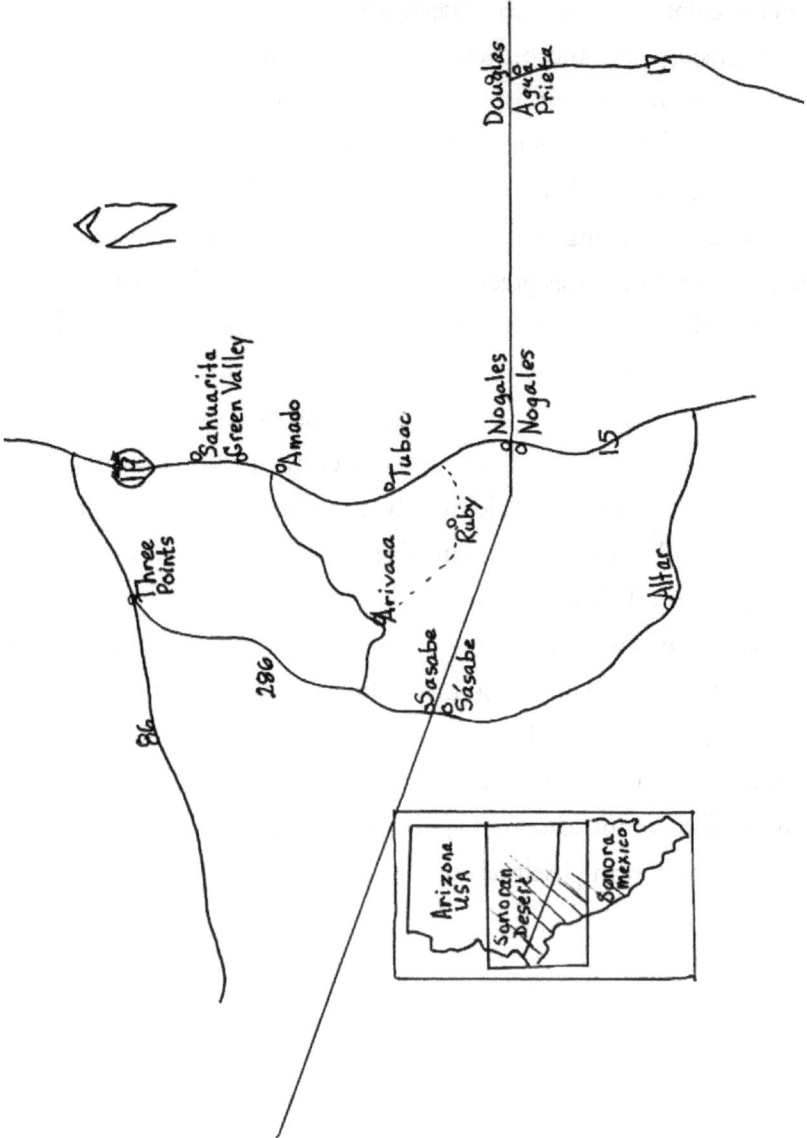

By Kathy Babcock

# CHAPTER 1
# COMPASSION

# Itty-Bitty Socks

*by Gail Frank*

There are no itty-bitty socks in the laundry bag. Just itty-bitty pink and blue tee shirts and itty-bitty grey leggings, stretchy enough to hold the chubby thighs of a toddler. This bag holds a man's fleece jacket with a label "Members Only" on the inside; some maroon athletic pants, a pair of jeans, a few women's tops and one pair of women's pink lacy underwear, a woman who has perhaps escaped rape on her journey north. Here it is, all of it, lives revealed in the garments of human beings fleeing for their lives.

It appears to be simply a bag of laundry, one of many the volunteers at Tucson Casa Alitas Shelter are encouraged to bring home after our shift of feeding hungry asylum seekers. I had put off doing the laundry, afraid of what I might find in those pockets. There might be stories of a life--perhaps a phone number or photograph of the mama they left behind or the uncle they are trying to reach. Maybe I would find a Bible verse that sustained them on their journey, or a crinkled love note of encouragement. In sifting through these personal belongings, I was looking at the last vestige of a human being's identity,

I had to ask myself if I was ready—ready to take on perhaps another piercing of the heart from the arrows of inhumanity. They had already suffered loss. Besides leaving behind their families and homelands, they often have all else taken away—their medicines, documents, meager supply of money, even their shoelaces.

I think of a story I heard about a man named Woody Carlson. Woody Carlson, a retired minister from a Lutheran church in Oregon, moved to Loveland, Colorado and started a mobile wash. Clients could drop off clothes to be washed in the large van parked in front of the library, then pick them up 90 minutes later, clean and folded.

Operated by volunteers, the unique and powerful Mobile Wash provides free laundry for lower-income families and individuals experiencing homelessness.

How interesting it is to me that it comes from the town of Loveland, a town that lives up to its name. The mission of Mobile Wash is to break down barriers to success.

Another inspiring story is told to me by my friend Pat Riley, a former Green Valley Samaritan whom I met as she dragged huge bags of laundry into the elevator at Casa Alitas, a shelter for migrants in Tucson, AZ.

Now living in Loveland, Pat volunteers at Mobile Wash. With Woody Carlson. She tells me of a young man who used the laundry service regularly and was able to obtain an interview and eventually a job, due in part because of his clean clothes. He now pays it forward by volunteering at Mobile Wash.

Volunteers accept, weigh, and sort the laundry each week and then wash, dry and fold it before stacking it for pick up. All of this, except for the actual washing and drying, is done outside where snowstorms in winter and falling leaves in autumn sometimes make their way into the bags. But still, the volunteers carry on.

Meanwhile, here in the Southern Arizona borderlands, I gently fold the clean clothes I have washed for Casa Alitas, including the itty-bitty pink tee shirt and tiny watermelon print leggings I hung on the line to dry in the Arizona sun. I hope the fresh fragrance of Arizona sunshine will lift up my fellow travelers on this life journey we are all on.

# Alma Of Ruby Road

*by Kristen Baldwin*

Her clothes are thick with the dirt and dust of the Sonora desert. Her eyes are pleading. I am holding my breath and waiting for the woman to speak. She reaches out her hand, and I put my fingers around her thin arm. She tells me she has an "hija" – a daughter – who is in

Tucson. She pronounces it "tuck-sun." I think about what has happened to bring us together here on this scorched day – she looking for a way out, me trying to help her find it.

She has been in the desert alone for two days without food or water, she tells me – hiding in an arroyo near a low-lying bridge. I ask her name, and she says "Alma" and something more, but I cannot catch it. I am holding her arm, and she is holding mine, as if she wants me to pull her into a lifeboat. She is utterly polite and respectful.

She wants to get into the car. "We cannot give you a ride," I tell her. I think of my online Zoom Spanish classes. We talked about festivals and different kinds of food and dress. There was nothing in the class about a desperate woman in the desert at high noon, hiding from the Border Patrol. She is begging for help. "No migra," she says. I am the only one in our group who speaks Spanish. Alma's Spanish might be as iffy as mine, as it happens. She looks indigenous; when I ask her where she is from, she says "Guatemala."

She asks again for a ride. She does not know, as we do, that there is no way out of this corner of the desert without passing through a checkpoint with dogs and a man with a gun looking into the back seat of our car. "Have a nice day" the man will say to us three white ladies. And I will feel guilty and ashamed for leaving Alma behind in the desert.

But I am getting ahead of myself.

International law allows us to give her food and water and medical help, but U.S. law forbids any kind of transportation or assistance in reaching relatives or friends. When I ask if she has her daughter's phone number, she reaches for a phone hidden in her bra. But I wave her "no," because I do not want to give false hope. If she gives us a number, she will think that we will use it to bring her help, which we are not allowed to do.

We do not know what to do. Food and water are one thing. Survival in the desert is quite another. "Thank you for what you do," the Border Patrol guy said to us that time. "You are saving lives. There is not even

16

dirty water in the desert now." He is referring to the worst Arizona drought in decades.

I tell Alma we will come back in two or three hours. We are searching for a bar – a bar on our cell phones, a contact with the satellite. We do not know what to do. We need to ask somebody. We need a connection.

It takes about an hour to get back to Alma. Her ankle is definitely swollen, from a fall or from whatever happened that caused a bunch of men to leave a woman alone in the desert. I look in the first aid kit which is mostly useless, but I wrap Alma's ankle in the way we all learned in Girl Scouts. I tell her she will be safe, but I have no basis on which to make this statement.

I do not think the bandage will do much for the ankle. This wrap is for Alma's heart. It is to show her that people care, that she is hurt, and that they are hoping she will get well. It is showing that she is not alone. I cannot imagine spending the night alone here, but that is what I am asking Alma to do. To wait. Until we find someone who can help her. Someone, not us.

To our surprise, as we are driving toward the nearest town, some 25 miles away, we see a white Ford F-150 truck coming the other way, with two ladies inside. They tell us they will stay the night with Alma if need be. Our driver asks that they call when this story has played out to let us know what happened.

At home, I let the dog out, a bit too late, because alone all day she had made some puddles on the floor. I fall asleep, but an hour later, the phone beside my bed wakes me, followed by knocking on my door. It is someone to say Alma is safe and not in the desert anymore. I burst into tears. Technically we have saved a life, but it is not like that. Rather, Alma has saved my life. She brought the faith that good people exist back into my world.

Thank you, Alma, for our time together in the hot and narrow ditch beside the road. 115 degrees is no joke.

# The World as Neighbor: A Conversation with Phyllis Hallman

*Recorded by Deanna Kleckner*

When asked how she became active in border work, Phyllis Hallman replied that she has never been good about not being involved. At an early age she was interested in other cultures and tried to see the best in people. She remembers growing up in Buckeye, Arizona, and spending time in cotton-picking camps. As a military wife she lived in many parts of the world. During that time, she and her husband Rod would try to integrate themselves into the local population. She has fond memories of their time in Germany and Greece and celebrating holidays with her Greek neighbors.

When she moved to Tubac, Arizona, an employee in her husband's company told her about a home for elderly Mexicans in Nogales, Sonora that needed help. The home was run by an order of nuns and headed by Mother Ramona. The nuns were struggling to provide shelter and food and needed financial support. In spite of the hardships, the residents were clean and well cared for but lacked blankets, robes, slippers and other necessities. Beginning around 2000 she recruited groups from The Good Shepherd to collect the items and to travel to Mexico to meet the residents. Over the years Mother Ramona became like a sister to her, often traveling to Tubac, staying overnight, and even attending the Good Shepherd United Church of Christ.

It was then Phyllis learned that babies born in Nogales, Sonora, often lacked blankets and were sent home wrapped in newspaper. Soon she was making monthly trips across the border to drop off baby blankets for use at the local hospital.

Phyllis even remembers transporting migrants in her car. When I asked her if she had been afraid, she replied that she did take chances, but if she was going to get in trouble, it would be good trouble.

She feels that throughout the years her border work brought her as much joy and satisfaction as it might have brought to those whom she was serving.

# The Bones of the Teenager

## Los Huesos del Joven

*by Marie Gery*

## The Bones of the Teenager

Fragile prey of elements
You came this way
        Air, earth, water, fire

Wrapped in time's cloak
only your bones remain
windblown into cacti
carried off, lost.

Your spirit called, waited
called again, again

Fragile prey of elements
you walked this way
        Earth, air, fire, water

Today we cry to wind, to sky
to each one named almighty
make strong words to free you
return you to your madre's arms

Send her your dreams, help her
reach you, hear your stories, your song
tell your brothers and sisters your name
She knows love did not keep you safe

Fragile prey of elements
you came this way
        Water, air, earth, fire

Your dream failed you
led you to this place
wind stronger than your back
sun hotter than fire
hard rain faster than the trains
Earth-danger all around

You came this way
Your spirit leads us to this place

Poem read by visitors to the memorial near
Jurs/Clarke property in Green Valley, AZ
where the bones of a teenager were found.

# Zapatos

*by Roger Kleckner*

The pickup and two SUVs are loaded and the seven of us are on our way to the landfill outside Nogales, Sonora.

We arrive at a wide area carved out between two hills. There were some large mounds of trash, but most of the area is dirty with windblown plastic bags and paper scattered around. On top of the hills are shacks made of corrugated metal, plywood, tarpaper and car tires.

We drive down into the landfill and almost immediately women and children begin to come out of the shacks and walk down to us.

While we wait for them to arrive, I look around: a group of four men are standing around a fire drum talking. Halfway up a large mound of trash, two other men are by a fire ring. They seem curious as to what we are doing.

We open the backs of the SUVs and drop the truck's tailgate. There are bags of shoes. We are here to fit the children with new footwear.

The women and some of the children are smiling as they approach. Other children look bewildered. The children range from about 5 to 10. It's winter and they are wearing layers of sweatshirts, shirts, T- shirts, and fall and summer jackets, though some have winter coats.

We line the kids up. One by one we sit them on the back of the vehicle. They are shy and unsure. Some have eyes wide full of fear. We smile and try to reassure them, but we speak English, and they don't.

We show them shoes, mostly walking or athletic styles.

We want them to pick out a style. Most are too shy or don't understand so we pick for them. One girl spots a pair of flimsy gold shoes like ballet slippers. Luckily, she's talked into a more practical pair.

How to determine the correct shoe size? We take off their old shoes. Some have only bedroom slippers. We measure the shoe size by placing the bottom of the new shoe next to the bottom of their foot. When we think we have it right, we put the new shoes on and test the fit to the best of our ability to see if we got it right. We are doing a pretty good job. We have some small stuffed animals with us and give them to the youngest of the children.

Many are standing and looking down at their new shoes. Some smile, others look deep in thought. I wonder what is going through their minds.

After a while the children seem to be more relaxed around us. They start to talk, smile and run around.

A boy, maybe 6, using a walker, struggles to keep up with the other kids, but he is determined. He pushes through a group to see what they are looking at and to get his shoes.

We have given out most of the shoes and animals. We take pictures of the kids with their new shoes; some smile, some don't. We have a group picture of us and the kids. The kids lean against us and we feel a connection. We are all happy and satisfied.

Later, thankful mothers lead the children back up the hills to their shacks. All are smiling; some waving back at us.

Leaving the landfill, we stop at a row of shacks. The people invite us inside where we notice wood stoves, dirt floors, worn blankets, cots, and TV trays for tables. Some shacks are selling items: candies, soda, beer, water and other snack items. Outside are fires in large drums. The people smile, happy that we stopped. They are poor but they gave off a sense of pride in what they did have. I admire their outlook.

# The Call

*by Randy Mayer*

Concerned about the suffering of those crossing the desert, I sought out like-minded people who were trying to follow their conscience and do something to help. I learned about the term "Civil Initiative." It is a principle that developed in the Sanctuary days. Civil Initiative is the legal right and the moral responsibility of society to protect the victims of human rights violations when your government is the violator. In essence individuals have international duties that transcend the national obligation of obedience imposed by the individual state. As a person of faith, I felt I had an obligation to answer a higher call because my own government was intentionally pushing vulnerable people to desolate areas where they were in grave danger. I knew I must rise up and do something to prevent it.

Among the Torah's strongest impulses is to protect the stranger. That is why there are no less than 36 instances in the Hebrew Bible of different iterations of the Leviticus 19:34 passage when God commands, "…the alien who resides with you shall be to you as a citizen among you; you shall love the alien as yourself, for you were aliens in the land of Egypt. I am the Lord your God." There is no wiggle room here. Boundaries are necessary, security is essential, but justice cannot be trampled upon, and hospitality is the grace that must be offered. Radical hospitality must replace cruelty.

Jesus as a devout Jew knew that he made the principles of radical hospitality central to his ministry. He was always either giving or receiving it. He came as a stranger into the world, vulnerable to the welcome and rejection of people. Without a place of his own, he acted as a host to individuals, small groups, and multitudes, making use of places that were available to him. He went out of his way to welcome, to break down barriers and borders to include and offer compassion---risking it all. With Jesus, sometimes he was guest and host in the same encounter. His practices of hospitality were always intense, personal, and counter-cultural.

We noticed that Jesus didn't always wait for the people to come to him. He would wander to the margins looking for the people in most need: the ones that society had disposed of, that had been pushed to the edge. He would find them and nourish them, treat them with dignity, and in the process they would be healed.

We tried to practice that same spirit of radical hospitality by driving an hour or more to the desolate parts of the desert to put water on the most active migrant trails. In the early 2000s, we couldn't put out enough water: 50 to 100 gallons and it would be gone in a day or two. We would minister to individuals or small groups of three or four. We never had the multitudes that Jesus had, but sometimes there were groups as big as 50 to 100 people. We were their servants, making sure everyone had water, clean socks, and a little bit of food. We would treat them with love and dignity. We sent them back onto the field, on to the trail with new hope and energy.

Because of these acts of love and concern, we actually had a protestor in front of the church for almost three years. He would stand there on Sunday mornings with his Bible and his placard. You couldn't ask for a bolder and more contradictory sign. It said it all: "Good Samaritan---Bad American." Try and figure out that guy's theology? Amazingly my congregation loved that guy. They would go out and talk with him, and bring him coffee. I wanted to put him on the payroll because he brought so many people to the church.

Our Samaritan group was a raggedy band at first, but we kept at it and people started to come to our meetings and learn about desert hospitality and civil initiative. Today we have 5 desert vehicles and over 300 volunteers that practice radical biblical hospitality all across the Sonoran Desert. For more than 20 years we have been offering hospitality and humanitarian aid in the desert. And we have had thousands and thousands of encounters with migrant brothers and sisters. We have found mothers and fathers with young children that have been in the desert for three or four days. We have found pregnant women, exhausted, nearly unconscious, ready to give birth. Last winter we helped a group of five cousins from Honduras that crossed a mountain pass during the middle of a snowstorm. Wearing only T-shirts, they almost froze to death. We have been stopped on the road by Border Patrol Blackhawk helicopters wanting to check our vehicles, and we have had more than our share of encounters with fully armed, anti-immigrant militia groups actively harassing border crossers and humanitarians.

# CHAPTER 2
# EMPATHY

# Seasons in Detention

*by Connie Aglione*

*(Reflections on conversations with 200 immigrants in immigration detention in Eloy and Florence, Arizona between May 2017-May 2019)*

The seasons don't matter much when you are in immigration detention. It's always cold inside summer and winter.

There are no windows to note when the sun shines or the moon or stars come out or go down.

There are no trips to the drugstore or Walmart to alert you in August that Halloween is coming in a couple of months.

No displays of skeletons, plastic pumpkins, costumes and bags of candy.

No driving down streets in December seeing holiday lights.

No visits to a church on Christmas Eve for mass or to kneel at the nativity.

No, holidays are like every other day and each season is the same.

Family is distant. If only a day's drive away, loved ones lack the documents to visit, don't have transportation or can't afford to take off work to see you during the very limited visiting hours.

All the family and friend celebrations you once enjoyed and that keep people close are kept from you. Sometimes this seems the worst punishment - missing the birth of your child, your grand-daughter's birthday, your son's graduation, your tenth wedding anniversary, the quinceañera of your niece. Maybe even harder, not seeing your parents as they are dying to say goodbye or being able to mourn at their funerals.

All the seasons of life, like the seasons of the year, have been taken from you.

If you are detained for a year, you will lose a year's pay. Your family loses all you do and are for them: breadwinner, caregiver, mother, cherished son or daughter.

You lose hope as one by one you watch the new friends you have made in detention lose their cases and be deported.

Still, you try to cling to hope that your situation is different and the judge will understand that you must stay in this country. You belong here. Too many hearts will be broken and lives disrupted if you are deported. Since all of this is impossible to contemplate you grab onto the belief that you will win the immigration court lottery. You will get to stay and be given permission to work and life will be better when you get back home and you will make things up to everyone.

Your child cries when you get to speak to him on the phone. He's mad at you for going away. You try to assure him that it won't be long now before you'll be back.

Your mother poured every ounce of love and courage into raising you. She's a single mom. The two of you were alone since you were a baby. She helped you make it. She worked. You graduated. You even won awards in high school. You're an American kid. And now tonight they unexpectedly put you on a bus at the detention center and drop you off at the Mexican border. It's 2 a.m. You lost your appeal. There is no legal way back into the U.S. for you. You know you have to call your Mom. But you ache realizing how much you are about to hurt her. You phone and assure her everything is going to be alright. You are OK. You'll work for a while and get the money to cross over and come back.

It will be OK, you tell yourself. You walk the streets that first night with no place to sleep. It will be OK. It has to be. You notice it's spring. That's lucky. Not too hot or too cold and since all you have are the clothes on your back, it's a good thing. Last spring seems like a long time ago. ICE picked you up on a night like this while you were driving home from a friend's house.

# Little Altars

*by Kathy Babcock*

*Tortilla cloth found in the desert by the writer*

Little altars populate the Sonoran Desert; some visible, some not. Ones I've witnessed include an empty gallon jug that once held not enough water. Precious, it was promising survival as it barely touched the relentless thirst of its bearer. Husbanding the contents carefully became a preoccupation that accompanied thirst. How long can the water last? How long must it last? What happens when it no longer lasts, when the jug is dry? Dry as the hard scrabble surface the traveler struggled across.

Another altar is an empty tuna fish can, label sun-faded and peeling, interior long since desiccated. At what point in the trek did someone open the can? Was it shared? Cans are heavy to carry so I surmise the feast took place early on. Tuna is good protein, but it also makes one thirsty. I lick my lips, remembering the saltiness.

A treasure discarded, an embroidered tortilla cloth with the word "Te quiero" at its heart, speaks to what was left behind and hints also at the desperation that made its owner discard it, now emptied of tortillas, but not of memories.

If you find one of these altars, you may take it with you, but treat it respectfully as its load is heavy.

# Courage

*by Gail Frank*

It's mayhem. Casa Alitas Shelter in Tucson, AZ, Saturday, February 11, 2023. Hungry people everywhere from everywhere. We volunteers enter the chaos. Today there are many young men from Haiti and India who request vegetarian meals. I want to know their stories, why they are here, but my job is to feed people.

One woman I will call "Courage" stands out. She is light-complected and has long, light brown hair. Though I don't know, I guess that she is from Ukraine. She is dressed in scrubs as if she just came from the operating room. I later learned that this is common for women to have their clothes taken from them and replaced by scrubs.

Unlike many others, she has nothing: no backpack, no plastic bag of meager belongings, nothing except for one thing, a baby, a toddler she holds against her chest like a sack of potatoes. The baby girl is clothed in soft-footed blue flannel print pajamas. She makes no sound but stares out at the world through her baby blue eyes from her perch on her mother's chest.

The mother wears a mask as all clients are required to do. Above her mask, I see only a deeply furrowed brow, the story of which I do not know.

As she moves through the food line, Courage motions to her baby as needing food too. We give the mother a meal and gesture that we will give her baby food once we finish the long line.

Later, I find her in a quiet place in the office away from the noisy crowd. She is feeding her baby just like any other mom.

After the crowds have gone on their bus to sponsors and things have quieted down a bit, Courage approaches me and points to the large box of cookies I am still handing out. She then points to her baby.

"Of course," I say, handing a cookie to her curly-haired baby girl. The baby takes the cellophane wrapped ginger cookie and examines it for a moment. And then, the magical moment happens. The baby recognizes what it is, and as Courage walks away, the baby looks back at me and smiles. It's a smile that fills her whole baby face, a smile that lights up the world. Even better, above the mask of her mother, I see a warmth in her eyes and the slightest hint of a smile.

Most likely, I will never see Courage and her baby again. But for the moment, our lives have bumped up against each other.

That night, I prayed for Courage, for her safety and the safety of "baby blue eyes". I pray for peace for this brave mother, enough peace to soothe her furrowed brow.

# Hearing Their Stories

*by Kathy Babcock*

T he temperature dropped from 90 degrees outside to a chilling 60 degrees inside the Eloy Detention Center. My friend Connie and I were led to an interview room by a guard whose keys jangled at each locked door. The doors slammed threateningly behind us. I no longer had a sense of direction but knew we were deep inside the prison complex.

Appointments were required, and we had a list of detainees who needed legal help and wanted to speak with us. These individuals were men and women who had been incarcerated for a misdemeanor charge. They faced deportation unless their bid for asylum or other legal relief rescued them. We were volunteer paralegals with "Keep Tucson Together", a free legal clinic for immigrants.

What we cared about first was trying to gather details to make a case for release on bond so they could return to their families in Tucson. We could help them build their civil case from there.

The first client was waiting for us in a very chilly room, overseen by an armed guard. Throughout the room were scattered other detainees with attorneys and paralegals all seated at narrow tables in plastic chairs. We chose a small table and three chairs in the least noisy area, as far from the guard as possible. Alejandro, age 19, shyly approached, sat down and began telling us his story. He'd been stopped by a Pima County patrol because he was following the car ahead too closely. And when he couldn't produce his driver's license, the officer called the Border Patrol.

Alejandro had lived with his undocumented mother in Tucson since they crossed the border illegally when he was four. Bright and good-looking, he hadn't begun to realize the danger he was in. A high school graduate, he'd only recently been trying to figure out how to earn a living without being a citizen. He'd never been arrested before, had participated with honors in ROTC during high school, and had strong recommendations from his teachers. All of this information would be prepared for pro-bono immigration attorney Margo Cowan who would represent him when his trial date was assigned and before that, would argue for his release from detention on bond. (Data show that 95% of the undocumented immigrants are deported if they are not represented by an attorney.)

Our next client, Renaldo, was a man who lived in a Tucson trailer park with his wife and two kids. He'd crossed the border illegally 25 years ago and built a solid life working construction. He told us he thought one of his co-workers called ICE to report him. One morning on his way to work, two large, black cars blocked him in at an intersection and arrested him. He wasn't allowed time to take his car home or to contact his wife.

Originally from Guatemala, Renaldo no longer had close family in Antigua. He had a middle-class life in Tucson where he paid taxes, owned his trailer and sent the older daughter to the University of Arizona. Another family would be torn apart if Renaldo were deported to a country he no longer knew. We teased out more information to support a petition for release on bond while he waited for a court date.

What would Margo Cowan, a pro bono attorney, be able to do to help these two men caught in an immigration system that never pretended to be fair? We wrote our notes as if their lives depended on them.

When we signaled that we were finished with the interviews, another armed guard escorted us back through the series of locked doors. He checked us out at the entrance, and we walked into the hot day, leaving behind the detainees in their icy quarters.

# Walking to Los Angeles

*by Deanna Kleckner*

It was past dusk, the shadows had lengthened and the lights were visible from the Abrego South pool as we were returning home from our walk.

"We should have brought a flashlight," I muttered as I stumbled on loose gravel.

We had just passed an arroyo leading to a riverbed when I sensed a movement behind a bush. Probably just an animal, I thought. We walked a bit faster but I could not shake the feeling that something was behind us. Nervously I turned around and found myself looking into the eyes of a small dark man.

"Por favor, señora. Do you have water?"

This simple request immediately personalized the plight of the migrants that before tonight were simply stories that we had read in newspapers. Of course, we would offer water. We motioned for him to follow us home all the while tossing thoughts around in our heads.

My first plan was to invite him inside and offer food. If we did that, would we be charged with aiding and abetting? Were we crossing a legal line? Would neighbors be watching us? How can being humane be a crime? I felt confused, anxious, a stranger in my own country.

I pulled myself together and went inside to make sandwiches and search for bottled water. Roger stayed outside with the man. In spite of our feeble Spanish and his broken English, he managed to ask us to please call a telephone number to let his family know where he was. Unfortunately, the number didn't work. He wanted to know the direction to Los Angeles and how far he still needed to walk. With a sinking heart we told him that it was a 10-hour drive by car! His face showed only a moment of disbelief and he turned and started to walk away into the shadows.

Technically he was only one of thousands of migrants passing through Green Valley in 2004, but he was a real person to me. I have thought of him over the years: Did he ever reach Los Angeles? What was his fate? Did his family ever hear from him? Could we have done more? Why were we so afraid?

Twenty years later all of these questions are still there for me. Unfortunately, the problem remains the same, if not worse. Today migrants have become political pawns. Dressed only in tee-shirts they are bussed from Texas and dropped in front of the house of the vice- president on a cold Christmas Eve, a gift from Governor Abbott. And I continue to ask, "Why?"

# Perdido

*by Jan Saunders*

Walking in the heat along the U.S. side of the border wall between Arizona and Sonora, Mexico, I gather up items dropped on command by migrants when they are taken into custody by the Border Patrol. Head lowered, eyes on the desert, I find the usual empty water bottles and tuna cans scattered among candy wrappers, mochilas, foil packages of anti-inflammatory capsules, pony-tail ties, gloves, and fake Mexican birth certificates created and sold by the cartels in Chiapas at an outrageous price. On my way back to the Samaritan truck, I pick up a child-size black belt and a single new-born baby bootee.

Later as I sort through my collection, I am touched by the worn appearance of the hand-knit bootee with tiny pink tassels tied in a bow. As I smooth it out in my hand, it crinkles. Inside, on a strip of notebook paper, I find a U.S. phone number.

I look more closely at the belt. Turning it over I find a slit in the leather that holds another piece of paper, another U.S. phone number, and the name Tía Berta. The phone number is missing a fourth digit.

CHAPTER 3

# EXHAUSTION

# An Abandoned Stroller

A stroller tells us about our broken border with Mexico.

*by Randy Mayer*

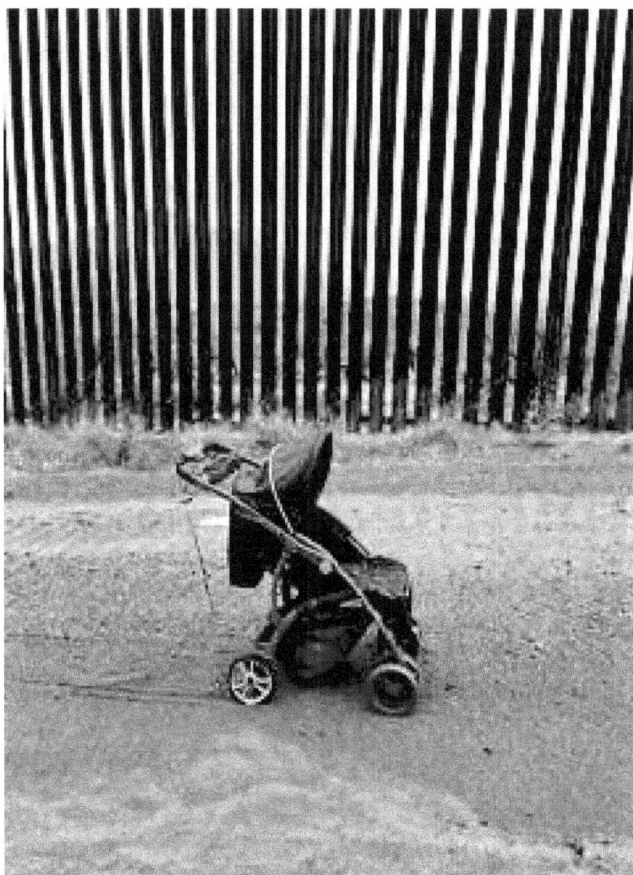

What we saw on a recent trip to the border is no different than what we've seen over 30 years: A mess that security measures alone can't fix.

We saw the stroller ahead of our vehicle, abandoned in the desert sand along the border wall. As we approached, we all wondered the same. Was there a child in the stroller? After 30 years witnessing the humanitarian disaster that is our border with Mexico, we knew a child might have died in that stroller.

We have known for a very long time that far too many children are on dangerous journeys with families trying to escape unsustainable lives in countries around the world.

They are delivered to our doorstep by the Mexican drug cartels — and make no mistake, every inch of our border with Mexico is controlled by gangs that now make as much money dealing people as they do selling drugs.

The cartels force migrants to cross the border wall in the most dangerous places, where they sometimes wait for days to be picked up by Border Patrol. Yet still they come, asking for asylum and hoping beyond hope for a chance at a better, safer life.

## Politicians make their propaganda tours!

If it wasn't such a human tragedy, perhaps we could step back and see the comedy. For as long as I have lived here, there has been a parade of politicians coming for photo ops at the border.

Their tour begins and ends with Border Patrol agents, who give them the standard law enforcement perspective as they share their Christmas List like 3-year-olds: We need walls, cameras, blimps, towers, agents … and the list goes on and on.

After years of these propaganda tours, the Border Patrol seemingly has gotten everything on its list.

Today Customs and Border Protection (CBP) is the largest law enforcement agency in the United States, with a whopping budget of nearly $25 billion.

## They say border security is the only fix!

Our elected officials, both Republican and Democrat, have swallowed the bait. After listening to just one side of the story, they are united, thinking security is the only answer to the border crisis.

What happens when CBP and Border Patrol become the primary voices Congress hears on U.S. border and immigration policy? We end up with an emboldened cartel controlling the border with a ruthless, iron fist, charging $6,000 or more per person to cross.

Not to mention a massive humanitarian crisis at our border and millions of immigrants unable to legally support themselves in this country. The cartels could not have asked for a more perfect storm of incompetency. America needs a work program instead.

And comically, the so-called "beautiful wall" that cost as much as $46 million a mile to build is useless, as it is regularly breached with a reciprocating saw.

CBP is so overwhelmed that they are now shutting down ports of entry and checkpoints, diverting agents to border stations to process asylum seekers.

It is long past time for our elected officials to recognize that security has never been the main issue. The people crossing the border aren't dangerous. They are poor, hardworking, family-loving people fleeing violence and terror. Money can't solve this problem. But policies could.

I would argue, in fact, that the very people who are crossing our border are the people we desperately need in the United States to fill jobs, build our communities, and make our neighborhoods healthy and strong.

## Trading asylum seekers for funding programs is simply wrong!

Get people out of the dangerous desert and out of the hands of the cartel. Create a work program to fill the millions of jobs that are open in this country. And, by all means, stop elected officials from touring the border with the Border Patrol.

I invite anyone who is interested in seeing what is really happening at our border to join any of the humanitarian groups that routinely visit the border to offer food and assistance to asylum seekers as they wait for Border Patrol agents to find them.

## Migrants are weary. We simply try to help.

As for the stroller we saw on the rainy Friday before Christmas? It was empty. We hoped that the parent who carried the child some 10 miles or more on our side of the wall, from their crossing point to the Sasabe Port of Entry, made it.

We saw some 300 migrants that day. One man came across our table with burritos and hot cocoa after walking over the top of one of the hills in the road. He leaned against the wall and wept.

# What We Looked For

*by Kathy Babcock*

As we crested the hill in the cool of the desert morning, I spotted what we had been looking for. Since we'd left Green Valley at six a.m., driving slowly south along the frontage road, we'd each kept a look out. A slight movement of a mesquite shrub or a flash of color in an arroyo could betray the presence of a traveler. Belongings——we used to use the Spanish word Basura until we met the owners. Belongings scattered under a bridge or on the roadside meant people had passed this way. Cheap cotton blankets, heavy with mud, evidenced the cold nights of fall and winter.

We eventually got very good at determining how long ago the shirts, shoes, water bottles, backpacks had been discarded. Clothing, shoes and backpacks deteriorated in the sun; plastic lived on and gave up nothing. We stopped the Samaritan Search vehicle to examine these finds and to assure ourselves that no one remained nearby.

We salvaged the usable backpacks, taking them home to wash and filling them with socks, hats, granola bars, and water bottles. These were the limited items we could readily hand to travelers still intent on continuing their journey. Among the items left behind we found fading family photos and bordados; the hand-embroidered tortilla cloths that revealed who remained behind, waiting in Mexico, Guatemala, or El Salvador.

Stopping at the Mercantile in Amado, we checked in with the proprietor, an amigo, who reported how many people he'd seen or how many Border Patrol were about that morning. From there, Arivaca was

25 slow-motion miles on a curvy road. The nearer we got to Arivaca, we knew our chances of discovering people in need increased. Sometimes the travelers made themselves seen, not caring that the Border Patrol might pick them up. Their bodies had been tortured by days and nights underway, by cactus spines, falls, and most deadly, blisters. They wisely and reluctantly knew they could not go on.

Slowly making our way through the small town of Arivaca, population 692, we turned south toward the border and Ruby Road. Still on the broken asphalt that would soon give way to dirt, we spotted three adults and a small child standing together by a mesquite shrub.

When we pulled up, we asked if they wanted to continue or if we should call the Border Patrol. The husband and wife with their toddler and a female friend with a baby in her arms said they were done. They'd crossed at Sasabe two days ago. "We didn't know how hard it was going to be," the husband said.

# Group Decision at the Border

*by Connie Aglione*

Four of us Samaritans were riding in the search vehicle when we spotted a man lying down just off the side of a dirt road. He was alone. We stopped to find out if he needed assistance.

We quickly learned that something was wrong. He was very weak and told us he couldn't walk anymore. His pulse was rapid, he felt hot and his face was flushed. He seemed somewhat dazed. All these, as we had learned, were signs of dehydration. He had with him a small bottle of murky-looking water he may have gotten from a cattle tank when his own water ran out. We had water with us but he couldn't manage more than a few small sips.

He knew he needed help and agreed that we contact Border Patrol. We tried, but as was often the case, there was no cell service in that area. We had to make another decision.

We knew his condition could deteriorate even further and left alone in the desert he would likely perish. We assist migrants under the premise that "Humanitarian Aid is Never A Crime" and will offer food, water, clothing, and first aid following those guidelines. But in this instance the first aid we could provide onsite was not enough. We knew that transporting a migrant in furtherance of their travel was considered a crime. If we took him in our vehicle there was a chance we could be stopped and questioned, even threatened with arrest.

We had a quick huddle and agreed that we needed to transport this man to medical help. We were not intending to help him evade Border

Patrol. We also decided to keep trying to call Border Patrol and 911 as we drove into areas where there should be phone service.

We helped the weak man into our vehicle and headed toward Amado. On the way we reached 911 and paramedics were already at the Amado fire station when we arrived. They assessed extreme dehydration and started an IV. The Border Patrol came while the man was still being hydrated. We were interviewed by them. We knew very little about the man except where we found him and the condition he was in.

The Border Patrol took charge and separated us from the man. We saw him emerge from the EMT vehicle where the medics had administered the IV's. He was upright and walking on his own, looking much better. The Border Patrol began speaking with him and one agent took him to their van. The other agent walked back to where we were standing. He gave us a warning about transporting migrants and told us it was against the law. We listened, feeling confident we had done the right thing in this situation. We spoke to the EMT's after Border Patrol took the man away. He was not going to be taken for any follow-up medical care. We were left to imagine what the next steps in his journey would be.

# The Things I Notice On a Ride to the Wall

## March 16, 2023

*by Deb Denison*

We left Green Valley about 8 am headed to Arivaca and then the wall. The sun was hot, but the wind was cold. As with most rides we exchanged life stories about how we ended up in AZ and in the Samaritan group.

The landscape along the drive is always beautiful. Today there were a lot of puffy clouds with the sun peeking out here and there. Many of the wildflowers are blooming and cattle are scattered over the hillsides.

It was Saturday so the farmers' market was open in Arivaca. There were signs saying that there will be a "turkey vulture festival" at the end of the month. That might be interesting to see.

We took the longer but easier road through Sasabe to the wall. The wall road is like riding a roller coaster, up, down, up, down. As we passed the Tres Belotes ranch and headed up that hill and then started down the other side, we could see the encampment, a scattering of several regular dome tents and many makeshift tents of tarps, poles, trees, rope and rocks. There are several campfire spots and a makeshift camp kitchen. There is a tent with food storage and a tent with clothing storage.

A variety of journalists were there: three from Central America, an HBO journalist, and an illustrator from NY. Two came with Christie from Casa Alitas. We told them to ask permission before filming anyone.

A group of women and children approached the camp; their faces show a mix of fatigue, relief and apprehension. We welcome them, offer food and water, and little by little they move off to one of the shelters to rest before BP picks them up. Camp gets somewhat quiet.

More travelers arrive. I notice a pair of red cardinals in one of the trees.

Some travelers were by Andy's van charging their phones via his Starlink (a true blessing) as they could contact family and let them know they made it here. He comes out here several times a year from the North-East specifically for this purpose. He also speaks fluent Spanish which is another great asset.

One volunteer, Jim, a very tall man, and a woman, Sister Judy, were busy cooking up beans and tortillas. The camp kitchen: 3 folding tables and several wooden pallets on top of plastic crates holding two camp stoves and a variety of mismatched cookware and various utensils. (I make a mental note to pick up a few more utensils at the White Elephant). Under the table is a stockpile of bottled water for cooking. Off to the side of the kitchen is a large pile of small water bottles for drinking. Behind the kitchen is the food tent with a remarkable variety of canned and prepackaged foods, fresh apples and oranges, juice drinks, plastic utensils, toilet paper and some first aid supplies.

More travelers arrive, mostly women and children and a few men. There is a camp cat that is somewhat feral but accepts all the food we give her.

The clothing tent was at one time organized, but not so much today. I eyed it thinking about that, but remembered my goal today was to collect as much discarded clothing as possible. So, after saying hi to everyone with a friendly smile, I picked up my garbage bags and headed out!

While I walk around I can see a few children who have eaten and rested now playing in the wash as children tend to do once they are fed and hydrated. I hear laughter somewhere. Someone is talking to his family. Andy is comforting a woman who cannot stop crying and has blisters on her feet.

The ground around each shelter is littered with blankets, clothes, shoes and various food packages. I see children's tiny toys, someone's shoes outside the tent, a child's coloring book with one crayon, baby diapers, and a tube of toothpaste. All of these are pieces of people's lives.

I picked up as many pieces of reasonably good clothes as I could. I shook a lot of blankets and hung them up where they could either dry or just air out. Travelers come to ask questions and we do the best we can with hand language, broken English and broken Spanish. Somehow I get the message and direct them to "the man or woman who does speak Spanish." Some ask where the "baño"( bathroom) is. I point a little further down the trail to a spot that has a few wooden pallets lined up to form a wall of sorts. It's an open trench with a little privacy.

More travelers arrive; it looks to be an extended family of grandparents, parents and children.

About now I need the "baño" myself. I know where it is and it takes me a couple of minutes to walk away from camp. It gets quieter as I walk. Walking just about a hundred feet or so, the desert once again becomes void of human chatter. Except for the wind and birds, no one would know there were desperate people just a few hundred feet away

More travelers arrive.

It's been about an hour or so and my feet and legs are tired. I sat down on a long drainage pipe and one of the journalists from Guatemala sits with me. We converse for a while and she asks me questions about the volunteers. She wonders if the Samaritans are a religious group so I explain to her who we are, about how long we have been doing this, and advise her to check out the website for more details. Another journalist who didn't speak English came along and she spoke to her in Spanish and smiled intermittently. She translated for me that he was surprised and impressed with the volunteers. His impression of most Americans, as is the impression of most Central and South Americans, is that we all dislike, even hate Latinos. I explain that there are some that do, but we do not and that there are many Americans who embrace diversity and believe that everyone deserves to have access to food, water, clothing and shelter. As we all got up to move around again, I had to ask for help as I was now really stiff and a little too low to the ground to get back up by myself. I don't remember their names, only their smiles.

More travelers arrive.

Again, I watch everyone going about their day whether traveler or volunteer. I am struck with awe as I watch the volunteers take care of people's needs. I am humbled by all of it, all of it.

Then I see a border patrol truck crest the hill. Everyone has been waiting for them to appear so they can surrender themselves and ask for asylum. I yell out a couple of times, "La Migra, La Migra!" Like a swarm of bees everyone comes to life, coming out of the shelters, calling their children and starting to walk towards the end of the camp where the trucks and vans will stop. For the next 40 min or so BP has the travelers line up-women and children and families on one side. Single men and women on the other side. All the journalists stand off to the side filming every detail of the pickup. BP took as many as they could, primarily women and children. The single men and women who were left are told someone would be back for them on the next shift, likely around midnight.

For a few minutes the ones remaining stay exactly where they were, in line and waiting. Eventually everyone drifts back to camp.

A few minutes later more travelers arrive.

By now I have several small trash bags full of clothes sitting along the road. When Kathy comes back we will load them in and go home for the day.

Kathy needs to go back to the end of the wall where she left her other two volunteers. As we drive along and are just about to get to our friends, we see another family group with someone who really cannot walk the distance. She decides to transport this person. So… I get out, she loads them in and now there are 3 of us sitting at the wall waiting for her to come back. The silence of the desert is nice. A few ravens talk back and forth to each other.

By the time we got back to GV it was 5 pm. My intention was to take a nap when I got home.

I was that kind of over tired where you cannot actually sleep so I fed my cats who were now annoyed because their dinner was late, stayed up until 7:30 and went to bed. My mind reviewed the day while I fell asleep, and the memories started again when I woke up. It took all of that day to finish unwinding from the day before.

# Water for the Journey

Dedicated to the No More Deaths Volunteers Convicted for Leaving
Water at the Cabeza Prieta National Wildlife Refuge in Arizona

*by Martha Jane Gipson, Laurie Jurs
And Ted Ramirez*

I am the walker who needs the water
Water for the journey
I am the walker whose body is failing
Water for the journey

Chorus
**Oh the water....Where's the water?**
**Water to carry on**

I am the walker who stumbles and falters
Water for the journey
I am the walker down on my knees
Water for the journey

Chorus
**Oh the water....Where's the water?**
**Water to carry on**

Leaving my homeland of heartache and pain
Water for the journey
I carry a vision of hope within me
Water for the journey

Chorus
**Oh, the water….Where's the water?**
**Water to carry on**

It's not OK that it's Ok
Water for the Journey
That someone dies of thirst today
Water for the journey

Chorus repeated
**Oh, the water…. Where's the water?**
**Water to carry on**
**Oh, the water…. Where's the water?**
**Water to carry on**

*Water For The Journey* was composed by members of a song writing class led by Tish Hinohosa at Common Ground on the Border, January 2019.

Humane Borders Water Tanks

# CHAPTER 4

# FEAR

# Fear in Her Eyes

*by Susie Sanders*

What was that look on Maria's face…desolation, confusion, exhaustion with tears? These are emotions I have seen many times on the faces of men and women recently deported to Nogales, Mexico. But there was something different about Maria… Yes, it was fear.

Maria and her 8-year-old boy entered the Mexican office of Immigration, just across the border from Nogales, AZ. She entered in a single file with 30 others…men, women, youth and families. Most were from Mexico and many were from Guatemala and other Latin American countries. The office staff process migrants before deporting or releasing them.

Our Arizona Samaritan group goes two times a week to welcome migrants to Mexico. We offer food and information about shelter services in Nogales, Sonora. I told Maria about the chance to go to a delightful family shelter. I was surprised Maria did not want to go. Something was bothering her. We did finally take her to a migrant aid center offering many services including pro bono lawyers to talk with her about the asylum process.

Two days later I heard she was at La Casa de Misericordia, the delightful family shelter I previously described. Later I went to visit her there. What a surprise to greet Maria now with a radiant smile and both of her sons!

Maria told me what happened. The coyote held back her older son the day Maria crossed. He told Maria he would cross the older son another day. She didn't know if she would see her son again. I understand why I saw fear in her eyes.

# La Bestia

*by Connie Aglione*

*Mural depicting La Bestia painted on the wall of a migrant shelter in Aqua Prieta, Sonora, Mexico Artist unknown*

The wide eyed five-year-old girl sitting in the back seat of my car was screaming, resisting her mother's attempts to put a seat belt on her. "This isn't starting well, I thought," also noting that I was going to have to get a booster seat. I'd made it clear that they needed to wear seat belts.

My friend Kathy and I had just picked up the two weary travelers at the Tucson Greyhound Bus Station. We had been given their names and knew they were mother and daughter but hadn't been told the age of either one.

As the child continued to fuss, Kathy was able to understand and translate for me what the mother was saying in Spanish. "She doesn't like being tied down. On the train I had to tie her with a rope so she wouldn't fall off."

Kathy and I immediately shared the same mental image of what their trip up from Southern Mexico had been. They had travelled for days on La Bestia, or "The Beast," the infamous freight train that several thousand impoverished migrants ride on top of each year to bring them close to the U.S. border.

The risks are great. We had seen pictures of some who had lost an arm or their legs after falling or being pushed off of the fast-moving train. Others died.

We'd heard stories of vulnerable migrants who'd been extorted for the "privilege" of getting on the train. Robbers preyed upon the vulnerable, often taking the little bit of money they had been able to scrape together for their journey. And we'd heard that people tied themselves to the train for safety. Of course, the mother had secured her little girl to the top of the train.

We slowed everything down. There was no need to rush from the parking lot. We talked a little about who we were and asked about the most recent part of their travels. They had been up all night on the bus riding from Texas where they had just been released from a family detention center called Dilley. They were tired and hungry.

After the possibility of stopping at a restaurant for breakfast was mentioned, the little girl perked up and allowed the seat belt to be fastened. I drove off. Over a shared meal we learned this was their first restaurant meal ever.

# Cat and Mouse at the Border

*by Deanna Kleckner*

It was after dark on a cold, drizzly evening in January as Rog and I began the forty-minute drive to the border. Our Samaritan group had decided to deliver cornbread and beans to returning migrants who were passing through the aid station on the Mexican side. It was a small gesture, but it would be something hot - something that said someone cares. For returning migrants already frightened, defeated, and cold, we hoped it could warm their spirits as well.

The group left their cars in a lot and unloaded the food in red wagons and shopping carts. Head down and peering from beneath the hood of my raincoat, I dodged cars and raindrops as we pulled our load across the road. Yellow headlights diffused the mist creating an almost surreal setting. We passed through the turnstile, entered Mexico, and continued up a small incline to the aid station, a small welcome tent with a random collection of chairs and tables, coffee pots, and a sign saying "Bienvenido." I remember how good it felt to warm my cold hands on the hot coffee cup as migrants trickled in over the next few hours.

From our perch on the hill, we could see the drama begin. Searchlights on the American side plied the gully that ran between the U.S. and Mexico. Their bright beams randomly stabbed through the darkness illuminating anything that moved. On the Mexican side these lights were joined by the flickering of flashlights. The protagonists were in place. Through my binoculars I could see the National Guard and Border Patrol in position on the hillside. Above us on an adjacent hill were the coyotes, men motivated by money to guide the action of the night. Their flashlights would signal the exact moment when their "pollos" would dash for the border, hoping to avoid the glare of the spotlights. I was watching a deadly game of cat and mouse on the border of Nogales.

When our shift ended, we packed up our gear and headed to the American side, an anticlimactic ending to a modern tragedy that would, unfortunately, play out many times throughout the years. It was an experience that I will never forget.

# The Quest

*by Carol St. John*

*Don't* go my son,
You *must* go, cousin,
*Take me* with you, my love;
Such words fell behind him
As cacti and scrub brush,
Dry grass and steep crevasse
Became the new horizon;
Sirens of hope until
He heard the iron birds' whirr,
saw their wingless approach,

He became a wild thing
Balled up beside another,
Whose stench he drank
Whose short legs did not run,
Whose blind eyes did not fear,
Whose ancient grit
Was the spirit he sought
As he breathed in the air
Of the javelina
Praying for survival.

# Visiting Altar

*by Jan Mason*

It felt strange. Drew and I had been sharing a bed for all these many years, but tonight I would have a bunk bed in the women's dormitory at the Catholic Mission in Altar, Mexico.

My sleepy brain mulled over some of the things I'd learned about the center. Part of its mission is educational. Since migrants come from various geographical areas of Mexico, they may have no understanding of the desert terrain of southern Arizona. The cactus growing in planters outdoors and pictures of animals, snakes, and insects are meant to introduce them to dangers they may encounter in the desert. A map of the United States with the location of New York City, Chicago, and LA is used to give migrants an idea of the vast distances when traveling in the States.

The next morning, our Border Links group walked to the plaza at the center of the city. On the way we stopped at a rundown hotel that was housing migrant families and single men. We entered the building, unprepared for what we heard and saw: many young parents with small children on the lower floor of an open hotel, single men in groups along the balcony. And then we heard a child's scream. A little girl was sobbing, clinging to her mother. She was looking at us, so fearful!

What had that child experienced in her young life that caused her to burst into tears at the very sight of us? Sister Francis, who led our group that morning, walked over to assure the child's mother that they had nothing to fear.

But two questions still remain in my mind. What had happened to that child that she was so fearful of us? And like that little girl, are some of our children on my side of the border also being brought up to live in fear of "those others?"

# CHAPTER 5
# HOPE

# Leaving on a Jet Plane

*by Val Chiong*

I was at the departures area at the Tucson airport waiting for my flight to Houston with a group on our way to Antigua, Guatemala for Spanish immersion classes and cultural experience.

We noticed that there were many asylum seekers also waiting for their flights to their families and sponsors. They stood out to us as we were shelter volunteers and recognized the ICE envelopes containing their documents and the cloth bags we gave out at the shelter in Tucson.

We began engaging and asking if we could help them in any way. I sat with a man from India who was traveling to his sponsors in Boston. He had been separated from his wife while in detention, and wasn't sure where she was. He had no phone, and was so worried because he had no choice but to leave her behind. They had already been out of contact for about a week.

I contacted the shelter to see if her name appeared on any of our accessible rosters, but to no avail. I let him use my phone to contact his sponsor. I gave him my contact information and all my prayers for his successful reunion with his wife.

We then parted for our separate gates. I received a WhatsApp message from him a week later stating that he and his wife had been reunited. He was so very happy and thankful. I will remember him always.

# Everything is Sacred

*by Gail Frank*

The nest the sparrow had been sitting on above my patio for weeks fell off its perch and landed on the bricks below. I got the ladder out and put the nest back under the eaves.. The next day it was on the patio again. I tried returning it one more time, but the wind blew it down. Too beautiful to discard, I kept it for its intricacy and architectural wonder. Tightly woven twigs and threads holding bits of paper surrounded a downy nest of what looked like soft dryer lint. Even a tiny colorful feather and bit of orange thread adorned the edge. Within a few days the sparrows had built a new home in the same place, and mother bird was on it.

The hooded oriole flashes its beauty in the Bird of Paradise plant after feasting on the orange slices I left out for it. The cardinal flits in and out of the feeder. The quail strut around with their feather caps looking for a parade to join. *Everything is sacred.*

On a trip to Safeway last week, a clerk asked me if I was a teacher. Turns out she remembers me from middle school 42 years ago! She said she loved my class and remembered my helping her. Now when I shop, I try to get in her cashier lane just to see her welcoming smile.

My son sent me a photo of my grandson who is on the autism spectrum. He is now 17. The photo is one of him and his first girlfriend at his junior prom. I smile at the wonder of his broad grin, one I haven't seen in years. *Everything is sacred.*

At the shelter where I volunteer to help feed migrants and asylum seekers, in the midst of the chaotic business of getting everyone fed, I am touched by the young mother with her baby that she swoops up and down to soothe. Another woman, dressed only in paper scrubs (provided by Border Patrol) bursts into tears upon reaching her family with her just returned cell phone. Still another woman, when served her food, first feeds her toddler. Another asks "Where am I?" She asks us to talk to her family members in Kentucky to tell them where she is. A young man from India asks if we have soap so he can wash his clothes. Another needs a towel so he can shower without drying off with his dirty socks. *Everything is sacred.*

If one lives long enough, like I have, now in my eighth decade, we can count on having had our share of heartache, loss, betrayal and grief. But mostly, people are incapable of not caring. Harry Belafonte, a singer/activist I admired from an early age, said his father taught him to always go to bed each night knowing he had done something to make the world a better place. I try to do that and remember that it's all sacred, and it all counts.

# Precious Cargo

*by Deanna Kleckner*

It was a dark winter evening as Rog and I headed to Tucson International Airport. We had recently signed on as volunteer van drivers for St. Andrews Clinic in Nogales, Arizona. Our first assignment was to pick up a group of mothers and children from Mexico who were returning to Tucson after a week's stay at the Shriners Children's Hospital in Spokane, Washington. We were to drive them to the border where they would be met by friends or relatives and continue their journey to their home, perhaps in Nogales or in other parts of Mexico.

As we waited for their plane to arrive, we paced and worried. "The van is pretty big," Rog remarked. " It's been a long time since I have driven something this size."

Since my role was to help with translation if needed, my anxiety went in another direction. Would my Spanish be good enough, I asked myself. What if I had to react quickly and became flustered?

Suddenly the sounds of children laughing and joking in Spanish exploded down the ramp. Clearly our group had arrived! The laughter gave way to organized chaos as the mothers shepherded their flock to the luggage carousel to collect suitcases while at the same time managing backpacks and stuffed animals. To many, they looked like ordinary travelers returning home. If you looked more closely, however, you would notice the adult-sized umbrella stroller, leg braces, and crutches. Many had had an adjustment made to their prosthesis due to leg length discrepancies or growth. Others may have had surgery due to bone defects, hip dysplasia, or club foot.

Our reception of the homeward bound was thanks to the work of volunteer coordinators at St. Andrews in Nogales and the dedication of doctors at Shriners Children's Hospital.

We pulled the van to the waiting area and one by one the group climbed aboard, not an easy task for those with mobility issues. One boy, 10 or 12 years old, in particular needed our help. His mother pushed him to the van in an adult sized stroller as his head lolled from side to side. His mother and Rog somehow lifted the boy and the stroller up the step into the van. I could not help noticing the adult diapers peeking out from his waist.

Once en route, the group began to laugh and joke together. The boy was accepted and included. Even though his speech was garbled, his smile told it all. Pieces of their conversation washed over me. I would not be needed to translate. Words were not needed to feel their relief and joy at being so close to home.

When we arrived at the border drop-off circle, it was late and dark. We helped them with their luggage and watched them cross into Mexico. They turned and waved a good-bye and disappeared into the night.

The road back to Green Valley seemed to stretch endlessly before us. Gone was the laughter of the children and we were alone with our thoughts and the black ribbon of highway. I could not help wondering about the mother and the older boy in the stroller. How far would she still have to travel? Who was picking her up? Was she the sole provider? What would their future be? Vaya con Dios, Señora, I prayed.

Gracias a Dios for the Shriners and St. Andrews workers, angels here among us.

# Velma the Samaritan

*by Randy Mayer*

One of our eldest Samaritans was a woman named Velma. Every morning she would walk her dogs in her neighborhood close to the desert. Probably two or three times a month she would end up bringing a migrant home from her walk. Her husband Al would always smile when she arrived at the door. He never knew whom she would bring home. She would say," I brought a couple friends home for breakfast." And Al would get busy making the eggs and toast ; the gift of grace and hospitality would begin to fill the room.

Hebrews 13, "Don't forget to entertain strangers: for some have entertained angels unaware."

Many Samaritans say they have met Jesus in the desert. Yeah, literally we have sometimes found migrants named Jesus. But I think it is a little more profound than that. Matthew 25 gives a feel of what Jesus was implying when he said, "When I was hungry, you gave me food, when I was thirsty you gave me water, when I was a stranger you invited me in." We all get that one, when we care for the least of these, we care for Jesus himself. But I kind of like this passage from Hebrews 13 a little better that says, "Be not forgetful to entertain strangers: for thereby some have entertained angels unaware." It has a little more mystery and love of the stranger to it. Rep Juan Vargas, who represents the counties close to the border in California, studied to be a Jesuit priest. His first question to people that visit his office in Washington DC is, "what is your favorite immigration passage in the Bible?" Wouldn't it be great to have more politicians that want to go to scripture over politics? We lobby a lot in DC for border communities and immigration justice issues. In my first meeting with him, he hit me with that question. My response was I told him about some of the angels we have met in the desert. His eyes teared. If you live in the borderlands, you have seen plenty of angels.

To be honest, I didn't believe in angels before I moved to Arizona. But I do now. I have seen them with my own two eyes. Their soft wings. The breeze that blows with and through them like a feather in the wind. Sometimes the angel is the stranger in the form of the migrant. Their strength, their pure commitment to family and loved ones, willingness to risk it all for life and love. That is the kind of family values that I can believe in. I want to be in a community with people like that. Not just a community but a world filled with deeply committed, loving people, devoted to faith and family. I will risk everything to help them find their way. But sometimes the angel is in the form of a Samaritan volunteer, a humanitarian worker, a lover of the stranger who is present at the right time and in the right place, providing basic needs in hazardous circumstances.

But more than that it is the meeting of the stranger and treating them like a long-lost friend, like a child of God, like they matter and you will go to the ends of the earth to make sure that their needs are taken care of and they are treated well.

Jesus had the great ability to be both guest and host in the same encounter - somehow flipping the roles. That happens often in the Sonoran Desert. Our Samaritans go out to literally save lives in the desert. But more often than not, it is their own lives that are saved - transformed, never to be the same again. If you have a heart, how could you not be changed?

And sometimes it is the migrant who is transformed. There, in a place of fear and need, they receive emergency care. Even when the Samaritan can offer only their presence, unable to give anything else, the migrant is overwhelmed by the love they receive. They had feared the worst. They had seen the hatred on TV, and that is what they expected. Instead they are embraced and blessed with compassion.

In the desert, on the margins, everything gets mixed up and turned upside down. Who is the stranger? Who is the Angel? Who is saving whom? And does it really matter? The only thing I know is that it is holy and sacred. It is filled with mercy and grace.

Isn't that how God's world has always worked? It is turned upside down, counter-cultural, twisted and turned, extravagant and generous. Grace appears miraculously when you least expect it.

It should be a clue for us as we seek to resolve our immigration struggle. It won't be found in the Halls of Congress or from whoever sits in the Whitehouse. The solutions are with the people who look into the eyes of the other and instead of seeing a stranger, they see a sister or brother, a child of God, an Angel unaware. May it be so. Amen

# Questions

*by Roger Kleckner*

A group of undocumented immigrants, save one, are sitting on the ground by the highway. The one standing is a young mother in a light blue athletic tracksuit. She's holding her young child, about one-year old. I don't think the mother's husband/boyfriend is with her. If he was, I would think he would also be standing.

Two Border Patrol officers are standing facing them, one writing in a notebook as the other looks on. They seem to be conferring.

Those seated look tired, clothes disheveled, many with their heads bowed.

One man in a stocking cap is staring straight ahead, elbows on knees, jaw set, determined, almost defiant.

Further down the highway a dark colored car is pulled over facing north. Two other border officers are talking to a man who is standing with his hands cuffed behind his back; his head bowed. A drug runner?

I wonder:

Was the mother on her way to meet husband/boyfriend in the U.S.? If so, has he ever even seen his child?

How far has the group traveled only to be stopped just over the U.S. border? How many are discouraged? How many are relieved to have been caught?

What dangers had they faced? Heat, cold, thirst, hunger, gangs, rapes, ransom?

I'm fairly sure the defiant one will cross the border again as soon as he is able. Will he?

Had the drug runner followed the migrants hoping that they would keep the officers occupied so he could slip by unnoticed?

Had someone alerted the Patrol of the migrants so they could be stopped to give cover for the car?

I hope to find answers. That hope is like their hopes, unfulfilled.

# Sharing Laughs and Hugs

*by Val Chiong*

One of my most disturbing and rewarding experiences took place a few years ago while I was volunteering in Tucson at the shelter operated by the United Methodist Church.

I will never forget the look of fear on the little girl's face. She was about four years old, lined up with her parents and others having just been unloaded from the ICE/BP van at the shelter. She was standing as close as she could get to her parents. Each family member was holding packets of papers and a plastic bag holding their few possessions. The parents held their children's hands but their eyes looked out in fear.

I approached this little one and placed my hand on her shoulder and said, "hello". The little girl cringed and was frightened, and I immediately realized my mistake. My act of kindness terrified her. How could I understand what she had been through up to this point? I was crushed to think a child would cringe at my touch.

As the families were being received, they were given a bowl of hot chicken soup, clean clothes and other needed supplies. After that they shed their fears like the water that washed over them in their first shower in who knows how long. They reappeared feeling human again, their personalities once again shone, the smiles returned, and a glimmer of hope was restored in their eyes. The little girl I encountered earlier that day is now sitting on my lap on the couch as we look through some books and laugh and share our love for each other.

# A Journey of Hope

*by Deanna Kleckner*

There are two roads leading out of Altar, Sonora. The first is Federal Highway 2 connecting Mexicali and Hermosillo. The second is a dirt road called "The Devil's Highway" by the thousands of migrants who often come through this small village on the 60-mile trek to Sasabe, Arizona, lured by the siren's song of a better life in the United States.

In 2007 members of The Good Shepherd Church were given the opportunity to witness firsthand this migrant experience. We carpooled to Altar bringing sleeping bags and pillows. We would be staying overnight at the migrant shelter run by the local Catholic Church. Dust coated our cars as we slowed for dogs lying in the streets. We found the shelter and were welcomed by the priest. Since there were no women migrants that night, the women in our group could use the bunk beds and showers. The men in our group would be spending the night on the floor in the common room. In the backyard, a display had been created with pictures to warn of all the things that could sting or bite in the desert. The priest explained that it was his duty to prepare and warn those who were making this perilous journey, many who were coming from mountain villages with no knowledge of the desert. If they had come this far, they were probably not going to be dissuaded, but perhaps this information could save their lives. Maps of Humane Borders water drops were on display and crosses and prayers for those who had left decorated the walls. As the shadows lengthened, so did the line of men in baseball caps waiting to enter the shelter. The doors would be locked for the night.

A simple dinner was served in the common room, and we were seated among those who would be crossing, perhaps tomorrow. In simple words and phrases the men tried to tell us about themselves. We listened and ached to convey our hope and prayers for them. Words could never tell the whole story. Looking into their faces and eyes was a much better mirror of their desperation and resolve. We hoped that they could see compassion and love in ours.

That night I tossed in my bunk bed feeling conflicted. In a sense I was an imposter trying on for size the trials of a migrant. In another sense it was important to bear witness, to try to understand and hopefully to communicate what we had witnessed to others who didn't have this opportunity. My hope was that with knowledge would come understanding.

In the morning our group drove to the plaza where human trafficking was doing a brisk business. The first thing I noticed were the vans parked nose to rear bumper that encircled the plaza. We would later learn that the seats had been removed and replaced with metal slats. The dozens of men who were squeezed into the van would have no springs to absorb the 60-mile rough dirt road to Sasabe. There was no shortage of vendors quietly hawking survival supplies: black water bottles, camouflage jackets, boots, hats, canned sausages, and bottles of electrolytes. Equally important were toothbrushes, toothpaste, razors, and all manner of grooming items to erase the smell and the dust of the journey that would help them blend in if they reached the United States. One item in particular stood out - birth control pills to prevent pregnancy in the event of a rape on the trek.

The priest took us to a casa de huespedes, literally a guesthouse, but in this case a flophouse where migrants waited their turn to cross. This was only one of many such places. Picture a cement two-story motel with doors removed, laundry hanging from the upstairs railing, and knots of desperate people standing everywhere. In the small patio was a cooking area where odors mingled with the stench from the single toilet provided for the complex. Across the street groups of men gathered in the church to ask for God's protection and blessing on the journey.

Later in the day we would begin our own journey, traveling comfortably back to Green Valley in our spacious van, our seats well-padded and the road free of ruts and bandits. My thoughts would travel that other highway, a path literally through the desert filled with potholes. A road where natural dangers mingled with the greed and avarice of men. With God's help, the journey would end safely in Sasabe where another more dangerous trek would begin. Vaya con Dios, amigos!

# CHAPTER 6
# PERSEVERANCE

# The More Things Change, The More They Stay the Same

*by Sandra Rooney*

Although it happened perhaps 10 years ago, I still remember the experience. I was on a Samaritan Search with Mike Casey. We headed out at 7 A.M., on a Friday morning, as we regularly did, first to Arivaca, making a stop at the Buenos Aires National Wildlife Refuge to use their restroom facilities, our last convenience for the day. Then it was out Ruby Road to Yellow Jacket Mine Road. When we got to the mine, we continued on, as the road turned east. Not far along, we saw a man stumbling down the hill toward us. We stopped to see if we could help him. We gave him water and some crackers and learned he had fallen and hit his head. Because he couldn't keep up, the "coyote" leading the group he was with left him behind. He had been wandering for two or three days, basically going in circles, only a couple of miles from the Mexico border. That's when I learned that we all have a dominant leg and without some landmark or directions to guide us, we would all walk in circles.

The man had been without water and food, and it was clear he needed medical attention. We tried to call Border Patrol but had no cell reception. We agreed among ourselves that we would put him in the car and head for the Arivaca Volunteer Fire Station, We stayed around until the ambulance came. We don't know what happened to the man. We called a Samaritan in Tucson to check at the hospital, but we never heard anything more about him. More often than not, that is what happens. Rarely do we know what happens to those we help.

No matter how times may change, some things seem to remain the same. Desperate people do desperate things, like migrants risking death in the desert, in search of safety and a better life. "Coyotes" still leave injured migrants behind. Migrants lose their way. It's difficult to have enough water for days in the desert, and there are many other dangers, not to mention extreme heat in the summer and extreme cold in the winter. Many die, more than 8,000 in the Tucson Sector since 2001 are known to have died because their remains have been found. The estimate of the actual number is impossible to calculate, but probably it would be several times the known number. We Samaritans continue to do what we can "to save lives and relieve suffering in the Arizona Borderlands."

# One Conversation with a Migrant

## by Val Chiong

I'm not sure what I was expecting when I volunteered to go help serve meals to recently deported people in Nogales, Sonora. The town is on the Mexican border divided from its American counterpart of Nogales, Arizona by a tall metal fence with razor wire across the top. I am pretty sure that I did not expect the brief experience to be a pivotal moment in my life.

The Comedor was started and staffed by Jesuit Catholic nuns and priests who recognized a big unmet need. Large numbers of people are deported from the U.S. with only the clothes on their backs and little or no money for food, lodging, or any other basic necessities. The Comedor facility offers two meals a day to people who are waiting either to cross into the United States or to arrange transportation back to their homelands. There is always a need for more help than a few church leaders alone can provide. Several area churches or other groups routinely help serve the meals that the nuns prepare. As a Green Valley Samaritan volunteer on my first visit to the Comedor, I was there to do whatever I could to help out. Between meal prep and cleanup, there are other services that migrants need. These include helping with telephone calls to loved ones, providing limited medical services, distributing clean clothing and toiletries or meeting with representatives from the Mexican Consulate. The nuns try to help prepare first-time crossers by explaining that if they are picked up for crossing without papers that allow them to legally stay in the United States, they do have certain rights.

At the designated time, the doors are opened, and travelers are welcomed as they file in. Men are seated separately from the women and children. Many seem sad and withdrawn. I wonder what they have been through during their experiences. I am sure they feel stress and trauma from being arrested and having their plans and hopes shattered. Some seem unable to speak.

Once everyone is seated, a prayer is offered by one of the nuns. I look at the sober faces before me. Many cry silently or seem to be very near tears. They bow their heads, fold their hands and squeeze their eyes shut as their mouths move in prayer. They sign the cross. The group as a whole demonstrates to me that their strong faith must surely be a big part of what helps them cope with their current situations.

Volunteers serve drinks and meals to migrants seated at long picnic tables. Typically, many of them are exhausted or have suffered abuse during their ordeals. Plates of food are passed down the table until all are fed. As long as the food lasts, they are welcome to as much as they want to eat. After eating, each person takes his plate to a waste bin to dispose of any uneaten food scraps and puts his plate, cups, and utensils into a washbasin. As basins are filled, the dishes are washed and rinsed, and dried. It is a big job and many hands were there to help out. Volunteers work on cleaning up. Several migrants pitch in to help. They express their thanks to volunteers and the sisters for their many kindnesses.

One of the things volunteers are advised to do is to speak with some of the migrants while they are waiting for various services. Maybe if they are able to express some of their thoughts and feelings by describing what they have been through, it could be a small part of healing and learning to cope with their new circumstances. I was nervous fearing I would not be able to communicate. Once again, I cursed my bad-decision-making, teenaged self for taking French instead of Spanish.

I saw one individual who looked to be in his mid-thirties, older than most of the others in the room. He sat alone at a table speaking with no one. His head was bent down and he seemed focused on something. I took a deep breath and steeled myself to try to talk to him. I was surprised when he replied in perfect, unaccented American English. He spoke gently and with kindness. Over the course of our conversation, he explained that he had lived in the U.S. for over 30 years. He has a family and owns his own house and has a business with several employees. He told me that he has never been in any trouble and that he makes plenty to support his family. This is the life he plans to return to. He cried when he told me of how much he loves his two children, a boy and girl ages 13 and 15.

In telling me his story, he said it was a morning like any other he had experienced countless times over the years. He had made coffee and went to his front yard to get the paper. Agents grabbed him and did not allow him to go back inside to get dressed or even grab his wallet or cell phone. He was not allowed to say goodbye to his children. He was dropped off in Nogales, Mexico where he knows no one. He explained that he has no living relatives in Mexico. He told me he plans to return to California. He seemed so sad and depressed. I asked how it was that he came to be picked up for deportation. He told me that his American wife called ICE on him. She has a new boyfriend and thought her husband's disappearance would solve her problems.

He said that he has to go back because of his kids. It was fruitless to try to discourage him from his plans to cross the border. I told him of the vast desert with harsh conditions. I told him that physically it is not possible to carry enough water to make it through the desert. He told me that he will travel alone and that he is able to carry 5 gallons of water. He has made the crossing before and he knows he can make it again. His kids are more important to him than anything else. This kind, gentle man, with so much going for him had had his whole life just pulled from him in one instant. This person gave me a whole new perspective on migrants. Each one has a story. I have wondered so often if he made it safely across or if he died alone in the desert.

# Streamline Lite

*by Katrina Schumacher*

The last Operation Streamline hearing in Tucson was in mid-March of 2020. Few people were sad to see it go. Every weekday afternoon in the Special Proceedings Courtroom of the Evo Deconcini Federal Courthouse, 75 men and a few women were brought in wearing the clothes they had on at the time of their arrest in the Arizona desert during the previous 72 hours. They had 5 point shackles on ankles, waist and wrists. At the time, many of the migrants arrived from Guatemala, Honduras and El Salvador and their small frames seemed swallowed by the shackles. "Evo would turn over in his grave if he could see what they are doing in a courthouse named for him", said his brother.

Witnessing the hearings was a visceral experience. The fear and weariness of 75 people straight from the desert was palpable along with the smell, along with the shuffling of loose shoes and shackles and the confusion. Half the men and women here were charged only with the misdemeanor Illegal Entry. They had never been here before; perhaps they had never been in any courtroom before and perhaps they did not speak English or Spanish--the two languages most available in court.

During the border lockdown there might have been the opportunity for the U.S. to rethink and restructure border policy but as court opened in late 2021 that appeared not to have happened. Low hanging fruit like DACA participants, non-citizen veterans of the U.S. military and parents of citizen children were still in limbo. The courts seemed to be groping for different solutions but gradually we came back to something that looked remarkably like Streamline. We called it Streamline Lite at first but it wasn't funny.

Today in Tucson--same Judges, same lawyers, same script, same sentences to same private prisons. So far only what Tucson calls 'flip flops' are being arrested--those charged with Illegal Entry AND Illegal Re-Entry--about 80-90 people a week as opposed to 150 migrants before March 2020. The look in the courtroom is different now as the prisoners, though still in 5-point shackles, have been incarcerated for two weeks and are all in orange prison wear and have had showers and new haircuts. The Spanish speaking attorneys (each with 4 or 5 clients) have had more time to explain the proceedings to their clients and there is less confusion. Some asylum seekers have still ended up here in a place where asylum petitions are not heard. Almost all are guilty of crossing without authorization into the U.S. for work and to rejoin family.

In the Tucson federal court, the busiest federal court in Arizona, there are about 350 hearings a week. Over two-thirds of those are migration offenses. Counting only the 9:30 A.M. hearings, each week you end up with sentences of about 14 years of incarceration costing close to a million dollars. Not only that but also lost is all the money that could have been earned by breadwinners now imprisoned.

# A Man Called Angel:
# A Journey from Venezuela

*by Gail Frank*

The U.S. State Department issued a warning that Venezuela is not safe for tourists due to crime, civil unrest, poor health infrastructure, and detention of U.S. citizens.

Imagine, however, that you live in Venezuela, where you can work as a bricklayer, but wages are only $2 a month. Your father is a teacher, and you want an education. You're young, 28 years old, but you find little hope of success as life becomes extremely difficult and more dangerous. If you fight against the political system, you are a target and soon start to receive death threats.

Like so many who become desperate with few options, Angel decided to leave Venezuela and migrate to Colombia where he had a sister. But the lack of opportunities there brought him to the decision that his only choice was to migrate to the United States and seek asylum.

And so began Angel's desperate trek, a grueling journey which took him six months from Venezuela through Colombia, Panama, Costa Rica, Nicaragua, Honduras, Guatemala, and Mexico eventually bringing him to the U.S./Mexico border.

With no money to speak of to arrange transportation, his only option was to walk. That meant he had to cross the Darien Gap, a dense 60-mile section of rainforest spanning Panama and Colombia. Part of the Pan America highway stretching from Alaska to the southern tip of Chile, it is the only gap and described as one of the most dangerous treks in the world. The Darien Gap is famous for one thing: ***things that will kill you.***

It took Angel three days to cover the 60-mile Gap while traversing the mountainous jungle, a swamp infested with deadly creatures, armed guerrillas, drug traffickers and hostile indigenous tribes.

The rest of his journey was filled with tales of kidnapping, terrible treatment, rivers that had to be crossed, and corrupt countries where he had to pay bribes in order to keep going. Combined with endless walking, the climbing of mountains, hitchhiking when he could, and taking a dangerous trip atop La Bestia (a network of Mexican freight trains upon which it is estimated 400,000-500,000 migrants ride each year to get to the U.S. border). At a shelter in Mexico, he was able to pass a credible fear interview and was fortunate to get the help of a lawyer who felt he had a reasonable case to seek political asylum in the U.S.

Hopeful for a better future Angel volunteered at a local food bank and other nonprofits while awaiting his asylum hearing.

People often ask us Samaritans why refugees and asylum seekers keep coming when the journey is so dangerous and life-threatening. Angel's story is just one of thousands of tales that can be told. With the growth in the number of international migrants on the rise millions will need a new country to call home.

# Slippers At The Border

*by Mike Nowakowski*

Ed Lord and I regularly did water drops in the desert between Amado and Arivaca. One week, Randy Mayer asked if we would take some visitors out with us. We agreed, but Ed told the visitors there were two requirements: (1) sturdy walking shoes and (2) willingness to walk to the highway if there should be car troubles. The Ford Explorer we were in that day had been flooding quite regularly. They agreed and showed up on time.

We started off with the three visitors and drove out into the desert. At the first water drop site we noticed that one of the visitors had on bedroom slippers. After trying to walk out for no more than twenty-five feet, she ended up staying in the car for the rest of the day. We were completing our route at the last drop site. The engine would not start. After telling the slipper lady it was about seven miles to walk out to the highway, she jumped out and began to dance in front of the car waving her hands and gyrating. Ed and I just watched as we knew if we just waited a while the car would usually start. It did and we drove to the deli at Amado for lunch. The slipper lady was animated and dead serious about how she had gotten the car started and saved all our lives. Ed and I said nothing.

# They Come

*by Sandra Rooney*

They come, desperate.
They come, afraid.
They come, hopeful.
They arrive, in the dark

Alone, in pairs, in groups
Men, women, children.

They climb high fences.
Or tunnel deep below them.
They seek jobs.
They seek their families.
They seek freedom from want and fear.

They experience
Burning sun
Agonizing thirst
By day,
Freezing cold by night.
They encounter banditos who rob and kill.

They follow the mountains.
They lose their way.
They are met or abandoned.
They die of heat or cold
Or snakebite.

They are helped along the way
Or apprehended, deported.
They will struggle on
Or return to try again.
Our neighbors across the border.

# CHAPTER 7

# REFLECTIONS

# Under the Wire

*by Marge Kinkead*

In 2008, as deaths of migrants were increasing, folks at The Good Shepherd Church began helping Humane Borders keep their water tanks filled to provide water in the desert.

Bill and I were living in Tubac at the time. We drove 25 miles north to the church to get 5 gallon - jugs from the bell tower, fill them with water and drive them 62 miles south to Rio Rico, cross the river and start north again.

We would park in a dry wash, carry the jugs, now weighing 42 pounds, down to and under a bridge and up the other side. At the time we were both in our mid 70s so I should admit that only Bill carried those heavy jugs!

One time when we got to our parking place, we found the railroad had done some work on the bridge and put barbed wire between where we parked, the bridge and the water tank. There was a body on the ground by the tank! By the time we had figured out how to deal with the difficulties we faced, the body had jumped up, realizing we were not going to do him any harm, he only wanted to use my cell phone.

We decided that the best way to accomplish our task was for Bill to bring the jars to the barbed wire where I would push them under the wire. Then we would get around the barbed wire at a place where that was easier and carry the water up the hill. Soon our new friend was helping move the water closer to the tank.

As Bill started to pour the water into the tank our friend began helping. After he had lifted and poured a few of these heavy jugs, he said to Bill in better English than he had demonstrated to that point, "How old are you anyways?" By the time we emptied the containers and returned them to the car, the man had disappeared.

Soon after, this tank was riddled with bullet holes. With such vandalism and with civilization encroaching on the area, Humane Borders accepted the Walden family's offer to put the tanks in the pecan orchards where they could be filled by trucks and we were retired from filling the tanks.

# Border Inspection

*by Dennis St. John*

On a cool May morning a Mexican border guard waved me over for inspection. As I rolled to a stop, a soldier with a rifle slung over his shoulder approached the window and said,

"Buenos dias, señor!? A donde vas?" (Where are you going?)

Now this was a question that I had to think about; I probably looked a little guilty while trying to conjure up something to say. After 5 years of taking Spanish classes at The Good Shepherd, I still could not answer a question with ease. I spent most of my time getting ready to make simple sentences but when questions were shot back in my direction, I normally responded with a dumb look or a word like "Si", which, of course, was usually inappropriate.

"Solo Nogales. Voy a la iglesia de Episcopal," I finally answered. My pastor had instructed me not to divulge that I was going to a shelter, so whatever I was doing would be blamed on the Episcopal church. The truck really did belong to said church.

I noticed two soldiers and a couple of other regular border guards walking around the truck.

"?Es este tu camion?" asked the soldier. (Is this your truck?)

I responded, "Es el camión de la iglesia."

The soldier questioned, "¿Qué tienes en el camion?" (What do you have in the truck?)

"Solo un poco de ropa vieja y algo de comida," I responded. (A little old clothing and some food.)

"Abre las puertas, por favor!" he ordered with authority. (Please open the truck!)

I fumbled around in the strange truck until I figured out how to unlock the doors.

About then, Pastor Randy called on my cell phone to check on me. He was also driving a donated van from a Lutheran church. It was also loaded with food and clothing. Our plan was to leave this van in Mexico to provide much needed transportation for the La Casa de Misericordia shelter. He had proceeded across the border five minutes ahead of me without incident. Our intent in separating was to avoid having two vans in a row that would appear to be a caravan. I said to Pastor Randy, "Uno minuto, Señor" And hung up.

Now I sat there thinking that this is not good: I had a little more clothing and food than I had just indicated. I was driving a 15-passenger van that Randy had earlier backed up to the Food Bank's door and asked that they fill the van with anything they considered extra that would help out our asylum seekers south of the border. In addition, Randy and I had cleaned out the vestry, the conference room and a storage room of all the old, donated clothing that we could find.

The soldiers opened the two back doors of the van and viewed about a half dozen crates filled with produce, boxes of other food and canned goods. On top of this were paper bags filled with donated food. And of course, the whole truck was packed to the ceiling with garbage bags stuffed with clothing.

They closed the doors and walked back to my window.

"¿Sólo un poco de comida y ropa?" he said with a skeptical look in my direction. (Only a little food and clothing?)

"Sí!" I said with exuberance.

He backed away from the truck and with a smile and a wave of his hand he said,

"Muy bien. Que tengas un buen día y bienvenido a México!" (Have a nice day and welcome to Mexico!)

# Windows

*by LJ Correll Menzel*

A trip to Ruby Mine was never on my Arizona vacation bucket list. But sometimes others want to go places and you are the driver. The four of us left our townhouse rental in Tubac and headed up I-19 to the Amado exit. Our map guys, Phil and Dick, were confident that it wasn't far. We exited and followed the roads to Arivaca. Destination: the now abandoned Ruby Mine. We were on an adventure and satisfying Phil's need to see an old mine. A retired mining engineer, he was determined to see this desert destination and we were up for it.

We passed through a border patrol checkpoint – a small set up with a few guys working the two lanes. We opened up more than the car window. Only a few seconds. Eyes more open.

"I wonder why that checkpoint is way out here. Hmmm. Migrants? This far from the border? Way out here in this desert"? I remember that my awareness of the surroundings picked up. What are we going to see? I wonder.

We stopped in Arivaca. Our timing was good because the little handmade shop was open so we interrupted their head-to-head conversation and chatted with the two women who were volunteering at this cooperative venture. We looked, picked up, put down, thanked them and left a donation. We walked over to the humanitarian center and studied the map that indicated that over a thousand people had died in this desert trying to make their way to the U.S. There were gallon water jugs lined up in front. In our mutual silence, I had questions about the who and wherefore of those jugs. Next, we walked into the little store to buy our own bottles of water, reminding ourselves that we were in a rental car and maybe we should have some water and a granola bar with us. All of a sudden, I was aware that "you just never know". Maybe we should be prepared for whatever happens. I think my shoulders got a bit tense as we took in more of where we were.

We followed the signs toward Ruby Mine and found ourselves on a treacherous, seemingly never-ending, pot-holed road surrounded in every direction by the vast expanse of the Sonoran Desert. I zigged and zagged trying to avoid the worst of them, happy I was in the driver's seat and not in the back where undoubtedly motion sickness would force a turn around. The worse it got, the more we felt far away from people, surrounded by nothing. Lurch and bump and swerve followed by more of that. I was watching the road but we were all taking in the desert landscape. And it went on and on. And way out to the south tall hills or maybe mountains. Every shade of brown and a brownish green – clearly not a welcoming environment. We wondered aloud at how migrants could possibly walk across this. The map was making sense. We saw no other cars on the road, but we were quite sure we were visible to others on a camera mounted on the back of a border patrol truck way off road.

What's that?

Watch out!

Look over there.

How much farther?

Maybe we should go back. I was ready but others were not.

And then the road narrowed and the spotty asphalt was no more. It was a bit hillier and we drove through arroyos, up and down.

Are you sure we should be out here?

Glad we are in a rental and not our car.

Where is this mine?

It is not far from here, Phil said. We've come this far. Just ahead.

We drove up a small rise and as we got to the top we saw another vehicle at the crest of the next rise. An arroyo separated us and there was a small amount of water in it. Dense with bushes and scrub right up to the road, it felt a bit like we were trapped in a tunnel. Do we back up? It was a big black SUV. I became a bit nervous. I mean, who else is out here? I know there could be migrants on trails back off the road but who is this? Are these drug dealers or something? We were at a bit of a standoff. The road was narrow here so we pulled as far to the right as we could. Slowly the SUV started down the hill, through the trickle and we stayed still and watched as they approached us. What happened next changed our direction – not on this road but in decisions we made about what we read, our curiosity about the borderland, and ultimately impacted where we chose to go to church and eventually where we decided to live. But that was yet to come.

As the SUV got closer, I could kind of make out a sign of some kind on the side of the driver's door. The vehicle had darkened windows but we began to make out a few shadows inside as they got closer. It pulled up right next to us, so our driver's doors were next to one another. Not much clearance between us. As if on signal, we both lowered our windows. We were all shocked to see four white haired women.

Hello. What are you doing out here?, they asked.

We're headed to Ruby Mine, chimed all of us together. Phil wants to see the mine. How far is it from here? We talked all at once.

Where are you from? the driver asked.

We're from Hayward, Wisconsin, we say. Our guests reply, Phoenix.

A woman in the back seat said, "Hayward? Near Springbrook".

Yes.

How much farther to the mine?

Not far, you're pretty close, answered the driver. Just a bit further. There is a guy there named Michael. He's okay. He sort of guards the place. He may want to charge you some money to get close to the mine. How much depends on what he wants today.

Good to know. Thanks.

And what are you doing here? I asked.

Oh. Well, we believe no one should have to die in the desert, she said.

We don't either, we all responded in chorus.

Well, good luck at the mine.

As their SUV moved away, I could make out the sign on the driver's door. It said "Samaritans".

We finally made it to the mine and met the guard Michael. Yes, he wanted money from us and way more than we were willing to pay. So, we made it there but then we turned around.

So many conversations have been fed by that encounter. Our backseat guests were very conservative so I was pleasantly surprised at their interested support of what those four brave women were doing.

It was the true beginning of our learning about the border. Our curiosity expanded beyond our enjoyment of Tubac and places nearby. Our winter get-away became way more personal and complicated.

We paid more attention after that trip to Ruby Mine ten years ago now. At dinner conversations wherever we traveled and back home in

Wisconsin and Minnesota, all our friends heard about our trip to the mine. We decided we could share what we were learning up north, adding our learning and experiences into a media vacuum. We rightly assumed that almost no one knew what was happening on the border. We could tell some stories and spread the word. It changed us, added to us, expanded our focus, opened our hearts. Our winter get-aways became more winter "get-tos" as we eagerly returned to this complicated place.

# First Border Crossing

*by Dennis St. John*

I had just turned 9 the first time I rolled across the border. It was 1951 and my parents had just experienced a long day's drive from Glendale, Arizona on two lane roads with me bickering with my 7-year-old sister in the back seat most of the way.

The family stopped at the Casa Grande Ruins for a morning snack of sandwiches, and I think we may have had a pop of some sort; we had an old metal army surplus ice chest to keep everything cool, but I suspect the ice was mainly to keep my dad's A1 Pilsner chilled!

No freeways existed to make the trip any faster but in the southern region there were things to look forward to after the boring hours of driving through the desert. Mom talked up the wonders of mountains and vegetation that were vastly different from the vistas she had experienced in the Seattle area.

We cruised down Oracle and through the City of Tucson; down the Nogales highway past Tubac and into Nogales, Arizona.

Crossing the border was simple; just a couple of small buildings with a shade structure out front that you drove through with the friendly wave from a Mexican customs guy urging us on.

Across the road there was another building of equal size that we would pass through on our way back to the States. I don't remember any gates, but I did see a chain link fence leading in either direction behind the two buildings.

I can't be certain, but I would guess it was the weekend as my Dad and Mom both worked. I was told that the weekend was the time to go to Mexico because the traffic crossing the border was lighter; the week was busier because of some program that allowed thousands of Mexican agricultural workers to venture to jobs in the United States on Mondays and then return to their homes on Fridays.

I later learned the program was called *Bracero*, but I only knew about it because I saw some of the men working on the truck farm next to our trailer park. My trailer buddies and I would occasionally swim next to them in the irrigation ditches by the big pumps; we never understood what they were saying but the water we shared was cool. We splashed and played in the ditch; the adult migrants took baths after a hard day's work for a little money.

The migrants lived in wooden sheds on the other side of the field without any running water or fancy toilets; I don't think they had electricity either as I never noticed any light at night. My family was privileged to live in a 27-foot trailer with a kitchen and Dad had even built us an attached shower out of salvaged packing crates.

Once we were in Nogales, Mexico, we visited shops that offered many kinds of enticements for kids; I begged for a little toy guitar, that I never played, and my parents bought some colorful rugs for the trailer.

We ate Mexican foods from carts by the sidewalk and I remember Mom buying me a 'white' candy bar that was probably made with mostly confectioners' sugar and sweet cream; I still remember the taste as delicious.

My family was not rich, but we were able to have extra cash for frivolous things that I suspect most of the people of Sonoran Nogales only hoped for. It seemed that the primary objective of the trip for gringos like us was to buy booze! Mom and Dad had a list of what other residents of the trailer park wanted on the cheap and the family was allowed to take a gallon for every person in the car back to Glendale. Dad was always willing to pay whatever was asked; Mom always bartered. I was nine and didn't notice anyone on the street begging, but I'll bet some were.

My job was to lug two half-gallons of *Oso Negro Gin* to the back seat. On future trips, I always got to keep the little key chain around the neck of the bottle that had a plastic *Black Bear* on it. Over future years, I developed quite a collection!

On the return trip out of Mexico the US Customs officials may have asked Dad if all the family members were US citizens, but, other than my dad or mom perhaps showing their driver's licenses, identification was minimal. Certainly, my sister and I didn't carry any paper to identify us as anything more than exhausted kids with mixed memories.

# Early Days with the Green Valley Samaritans

*By Judith Whipple*

J oining the Green Valley/Sahuarita Samaritans in 2005 was a life-changing experience for me. It was modeled by its co-founders on the distinguished role of the Tucson Samaritans who were already active on Arizona's border.

For starters, we learned that only roughly 8% of the world's population have never been hungry and always had a roof overhead. At the U.S. southern border, migrants from Mexico, Central and South America arrived to tell a different story. We served the Tucson Sector.

On the cover of our yellow brochure was the mission statement "To Save Lives and Relieve Suffering in the Arizona Borderlands." We had two major tasks: 1) driving marked Search vehicles each day to roads near known migrant trails, Arivaca an important way station, and 2) aiding deported migrants under a tent behind the Mariposa Port of Entry customs building in Nogales, Sonora.

We learned to observe circling vultures; to call Borstar for a migrant in medical trouble; the significance of cloth-covered shoes; to identify why a Border Patrol vehicle dragged a car tire behind it on dirt trails and roads and what a "lay-up" site meant. Armed with rudimentary Spanish, we would park our Search cars and walk into washes big and small, calling out "Somos amigos," "Como esta?", "Tenemos agua y comida," "Necesita ayuda?" to urge migrants to show themselves.

It was a time when Border Patrol separated men from their families, and delivered their wives, mothers and children back across the border in the middle of the night, to "The Tent" behind the Mariposa customs building. There was one water spigot. There were no cots for the weary until many months later. About two years later, the Mexican government parked a big tourist-type bus behind the tent, signaling medical help; it was rarely staffed.

Each Tuesday morning, Samaritans would cross the border carrying food, water, medical supplies, clothes, and small plastic bins in which to wash damaged, weary feet. Cartel members—"coyotes"— would crouch on a nearby ridge looking down into our tent, and one day easily persuaded an unusually beautiful migrant woman, after we'd washed and treated her feet, to join them.

One small woman with a two-month old baby girl sat exhausted in one of the few chairs. She was indigenous, and spoke no Spanish. It was January, cold and rainy. The baby had no shoes or socks on her tiny perfect feet, and wailed when she went into our arms so her mother could down a bowl of Top Ramen.

Eventually a permanent aid station was established in a small rough building about a half mile beyond the tent complete with a small kitchen and incredibly, two toilets!

# All in a Day

*by Betsy Schatz Smith*

His parents brought him as a young boy to the United States from Nicaragua. He lived and went to school here for 20 years but always yearned to go back to his birth country. When he returned to his homeland he found he couldn't live under the turmoil of that government. Unfortunately, with no legal way to return, he walked most of the way to the Mexican U.S. border and asked for asylum. He's now on his way back to his family in the United States.

A family with 2 parents, a teenager who spoke English and a young son, arrived at the migrant shelter from India. As they were eating lunch, I noticed them looking at the United States map hanging on the wall. I asked the teenager where they were heading. They were heading to Alabama where they have family. I showed them where they were in Arizona and how far away Alabama is. The kids were excited, but I could see from the mom's eyes that she understood they still had a long way to go.

A young man, Carlos, along with his uncle and 2 cousins arrived from Venezuela. They walked most of the way including through the Darian Gap. It took them almost 4 months to reach the U.S. They are heading to Miami where a sister lives. They've been at the shelter for over a week now. Carlos wants to keep busy and also practice his English so he's volunteering in the lunchroom. He helps by sanitizing migrants' hands before they enter for lunch and answers migrants' questions which is helpful to most of us who speak very little Spanish.

Lunch is almost over and people are beginning to clear out. One large family is still sitting. One of the men motions he would like another sandwich for his wife. Then he rubs her tummy. She looked embarrassed, got up from the table and started helping us sanitize the lunchroom tables. The next day when I arrived to volunteer in the lunchroom, I'm told a woman fainted twice. EMT's were called and they wanted to take her to the hospital, but she refused. It turns out it's the same young woman who helped yesterday cleaning up after lunch. She's pregnant but not showing yet. Our guess is she didn't want to go to the hospital for fear she'd be separated from her husband and family.

It amazes me how resilient the children are. It's fun and interesting to watch the migrant children who have no toys make up games. One small group of 5 boys, probably 6-8 years old, were kicking an empty water bottle pretending it was a soccer ball which brought lots of smiles and laughter. They had cleared space in the sleeping area for the game. Two youngsters, 3-5 years old, hopped from one floor tile to another without stepping on the lines.

A baby from Senegal was crying uncontrollably and couldn't be quieted. I gave the mom an empty water bottle for the baby to squeeze. The noise it made was a good substitute for a rattle. It worked in calming the baby and the mom gave a big sigh of relief.

After lunch was nearly over, Susana, the woman custodian, came in and sat down. She was rubbing her arm and shoulder because she had pulled some muscles and they were sore. An older South American man walked over and motioned he wanted to touch her arm or shoulder. He kept on insisting and reluctantly she let him rub and manipulate her arm. Turns out he was a chiropractor in Columbia.

This story brings me to tears just remembering it. A bus from the border dropped off 40-50 Spanish speaking people, An older man walked in, sat down and started sobbing. He wouldn't talk, didn't want any food, and wouldn't make eye contact, We volunteers felt so helpless. A few hours later another bus arrived with a similar group. Suddenly the man jumped up, ran over and started hugging a young woman and 2 smaller children. We assumed she was his daughter with his grandchildren. Our guess is they were separated at the border and had no idea if they'd see each other again.

A young man from Guatemala hands me his phone which has the translator app. He wants to know where he is. I say Tucson, Arizona. He thought he was in California which is where he's heading. He and his wife were separated at the border, and he's lost contact with her. He thinks her cell phone is either lost or needs to be charged, and she doesn't have a charging cord. He's frantic to locate her. This is just another situation which makes me feel so helpless.

# Four Hours at the Drexel Center

*by SuEllen Shaw*

Migrants asking for Humanitarian Parole or seeking asylum are delivered by ICE and the US Border Patrol. With that delivery, they arrive legally and from there go to their family, friends, or sponsors across the U.S. I volunteer at the Drexel Center in Tucson, AZ, where people in the country await their court dates. If transportation is not immediately available, single males stay at the Drexel, families and single women may go to Casa Alitas, the Ramada, or the Quality Inn, while people testing positive for Covid go to the Red Roof Inn.

Driving through the gate of the Drexel Center, I see on my right the two huge trailers holding eight showers each. There is usually a line of men waiting their turn for a stall. On my left, surrounding the parking lot and grounds, are 6' high chain link fences, topped with concertina wire. Trees reach over the fence, but offer little shade from the burning Arizona sun. Across the fence and beyond the tree branches, hangs the laundry in all its colors and shapes. There are no clothes pins. Draped across and through the holes, shirts, boxer shorts, trousers, sneakers, socks, blankets, and towels stir in the hot breeze. Meanwhile, their owners stand or sit under other trees that line the various parking areas, offering a bit of shade. They keep watch on their laundry and talk, wait, plan, smoke.

The men do their laundry in the showers, as they shower. Their actions and attempts to be clean in hard conditions belie the stereotype of "dirty immigrant." In all my weeks serving lunches at the Center, I have yet to notice a man's body odor, whether he is from Mexico, Guatemala, Ecuador, El Salvador, Venezuela, Columbia, Georgia, Afghanistan,

137

Pakistan, India, Chad, South Africa, Mauritania, Senegal, Haiti or the many other countries that contribute to migration and traffic through the Drexel.

Parking my car, I walk with three other Green Valley volunteers into the center. We sign in, stating our volunteer area: I sign up for lunch service. We are carefully vetted and wear our official name tags with our pictures so that permanent staff and residents know we can be there.

A make-shift hallway has been created with the fabric walls used to create cubicles in large offices. That 70' long wall on our left, along which we walk to the dining room, separates us from the men's dormitory of 170 cots. Each guest has received a gray and red blanket from the Red Cross. Those blankets splay across cots. Some cover resting men sleeping or studying their phones; others are tossed and lay claim to the cot that someone has left for a short time. Both under the blankets and under the cots are the blue bags issued to the men as they arrive. The bags contain clean socks, underwear, a hat, toiletry items, some of their own personal belongings, etc. However, many of the guests keep their packs near them, trying to secure what little they have. There are no lockers, no storage closets, no secure bins available.

On our right we pass another line of men waiting at the window of the clothes closet, a large room dedicated to donated clothing, shoes, etc. Lydia, another volunteer, gives the men what they ask for if she has it. A common request is for shoelaces because the Border Patrol takes their shoelaces when they enter the country.

Making our way along the hallway, we pass many men talking on their phones, some presumably reassuring those at home that they have reached the United States and await transportation. That transport to the airport, bus terminal, or train where they will be transported to their sponsors, friends, or family across the country is provided by other volunteers and by the Tucson transit system. Other guests contact family and friends, looking for news of home. Some cluster in groups, obviously reassuring each other, supporting one another with quiet conversation, sometimes laughing over jokes together. I continue to be amazed at the smiles and good humor many have after what they have endured to get this far.

When we reach the dining hall, our work begins. We divide the tasks among us. But first we follow the hand washing and rubber glove routine, then get our aprons. Today, I gather, sanitize, and refill the eight five-gallon water igloos from around the center. Three belong in the dining room. I return the others around the center: two to large family rooms where families await their transportation; one to the medical center where newly arrived guests are tested for covid or treated for other conditions; two to the intake area where guests register and get arrangements for transportation and housing.

When the three food cages from the World Dining catering company arrive, the other volunteers move the box lunches and dinners into huge commercial refrigerators, making sure to pay attention to and arrange them by expiration date. The most recently delivered meals get served last. Each food cage holds 500 boxes. Moving and arranging takes at least half an hour. Today we will serve 200 lunches. It is not uncommon to serve up to 300. Preparing the dining hall, filling the napkin holders, washing apples, arranging the buffet line with the boxed lunches, extra cookies, chips, and apples takes about an hour.

We volunteers divide the serving duties as we prepare to open the doors for the waiting lunch line outside. Two of us greet at the door, one dispensing hand sanitizer, the other checking arrival dates on the guests' official entry packets. To receive lunch, they must have spent the night. Those arriving that morning have received a breakfast box and must wait until dinner for another meal. The next volunteer hands out the lunch boxes, offering a vegetarian or a meat option, necessary in respect of others' dietary restrictions. I have learned several new words to distinguish between the two boxed options, as I point at each: carne, pollo, viande, halal. Each box contains a sandwich, an apple, chips, a cookie, and a mayonnaise packet. The next volunteer hands out water cups and invites guests to take extra apples, chips, or cookies. If we have enough volunteers, the last person floats, refilling the food line, making necessary announcements regarding table bussing, etc., cleaning tables as guests leave or mingling and answering questions when possible.

After the guests finish their lunch, we restore the dining room to order, readying it for the volunteers coming in later to serve dinner. The whole process from starting to finishing our shift takes about four hours, a small amount of time next to the journey and quest for freedom, safety, and a chance to earn a living that these men have experienced.

# CHAPTER 8

# RESPECT

# It Takes a Village

*by Gail Frank*

The African proverb, "It Takes a Village," is often quoted to mean that *an entire community of people must interact with children for those children to experience and grow in a safe and healthy environment.* And so it is with Green Valley/Sahuarita Samaritans in their border work for asylum seekers.

When it comes to boots-on-the-ground activities like providing food, water, clothing, medical assistance and shelter, that is when the village really comes to life.

"What can we do to help?" volunteers ask. "What do you need?" The answers are specific and varied like, "we need flip-flops." Or "we need socks." Most immigrants have walked hundreds of miles and their feet are blistered. Some cannot fit their bandaged feet back into their shoes.

We need water. We never have enough water. We need blankets, coloring books for kids, and medical supplies. We need taxi or bus fare to get folks safely from the port of entry drop-offs to Kino Border Initiative where they can be fed, hydrated, shower and make arrangements for transport to Casa Alitas shelter in Tucson where they will go to their sponsors.

Yes, the government is doing what it can, but the wheels of justice and change grind slowly. Lawmakers are working on policy, looking at root causes. But it is the village that is doing the work in the meantime. It is the humanitarian groups like No More Deaths, The Florence Project, Humane Borders, The Tucson and Green Valley Samaritans, the Red Cross, and the shelter systems in Arizona, Texas, and Mexico that are doing the village work. They are bandaging feet, providing food and water, a safe haven to rest, coloring books and crayons for children and transportation to shelters and families. The most important gift the village provides is respect, acceptance, and the offering of dignity by a welcoming smile and a listening ear.

Like most efforts of networking, for the village to work, it takes good relationships. Greg Mortenson, inspired by impoverished mountain villagers in Pakistan, wrote a book in 1993 entitled *Three Cups of Tea*. His premise was that before you try to rectify any situation, before you jump in with your directives and solutions, you first sit down and share a cup of tea. Then the work begins.

Indeed, it does take a village. Whether it's flip flops, taxi fare, a pot of beans and rice or a simple welcoming smile, we, the village, come to the fray and offer what we can. "They" are not coming to save us. "We" are the ones we've been waiting for. We are the village.

# Deep Lessons in Hospitality

*by Laurie Jurs*

*The Arabs used to say,*
*When a stranger appears at your door,*
*feed him for three days before asking who he is,*
*where he has come from or where he's headed.*
*That way, he'll have strength enough to answer.*
*Or, by then you'll be such good friends you don't care.*

*Red Brocade* by Naomi Shihab Nye

With these words, we prepared for the 12th Annual Migrant Trail. Fifty-nine of us, from around the country, Canada, Colombia, Mexico and Central America set out on the last week of May to walk 75 miles in the footsteps of desert crossers from Sasabe, Sonora, Mexico to Kennedy Park in southwest Tucson.

Not a fundraiser, athletic event or protest march, it was a pilgrimage in honor of those who have crossed and those who did not make it across. For me, there were deep lessons in hospitality.

Mennonites, Quakers and Catholics, among others, made up our group. These faith communities have traditions of welcoming the stranger, of lives of service, of being hospitable, not only providing hospitality. What I heard from one Mennonite stuck with me. He said, "The opposite of violence is not non-violence. The opposite of violence is hospitality."

I looked up the word's origin. It comes from the Latin root "hospes" which means guest, host and stranger. What a fascinating linguistic intertwining. Each needs the other to exist.

What forms of hospitality did I see on the Migrant Trail? There was the openhearted welcome to us first timers from the Walk veterans, from showing us our jobs (mine included the pop-up outhouses) to preparing us for the emotional rollercoaster to come.

There was sustenance from the many church and humanitarian groups that brought us meals and water throughout the week. (The Green Valley/Sahuarita Samaritans have made a high holy art form of this.)

There was the body and soul satisfying overnight at Serenity Baptist Church in Three Points. Real tables and chairs made the Thai banquet brought by a Buddhist fellowship from Tucson especially enjoyable. A saffron-robed monk led us in a prayer of gratitude.

But what of the hospitality shown or not shown to the desert crossers themselves? A few weeks before the Walk, an exhausted migrant knocked on a friend's door near Green Valley. She gave him food, drink and a safe place to rest a minute. Though she speaks little Spanish, she has asked God and his guardian angels to send anyone lost and suffering to her. She asked for my help with Spanish. We learned he and two cousins had crossed near Sasabe, walking 10 days to reach Green Valley. We gave them kindness and sustenance and wished them Godspeed.

I walked a similar route to theirs, taking seven days. I had food, water, a sleeping bag and most importantly, a safety net. I knew where I was and what lay ahead. And it was still damned difficult. Not all of us finished the Walk nor walked the whole way. But none of us died.

For lack of hospitality, many have anguished and perished not far from our own communities. There are three sites a short walk from my own home in southern Green Valley, where we found the bones of migrants. We marked them with crosses that read "Desconocido" or "Unknown."

We carried simple white crosses on the Walk. I selected one marked "Desconocido," of which there were many. Other crosses had names painted on them, names of people that have been identified.

How do you show hospitality to the dead? Our trek became a funeral procession when we walked single file in silence. Periodically, the quiet would be broken by a leader shouting a name or "Desconocido" or "Desconocida", each one followed by a group shout-out of "Presente!" We know you lived. We know you died here. We know your spirit lives on and we will never forget you.

People developed relationships with their crosses over the week. Jorge from Agua Prieta said he felt he'd helped a lost soul named Jose finish his journey, helped him get to Tucson. The nurse from Calgary started out carrying one cross, immediately developing a sharp neck pain, one she'd never had before. A few days later, she acquired a second cross and the pain vanished. It came to me that maybe those two people knew each other, somehow, some way.

At our closing circle beneath a bluff by Kinney Road and Ajo Way, with five great horned owls looking on, we held out our crosses for a sprinkle of water. "Here, Desconocido, it's way too little and way too late, but here's some water for you. Here's some water for you, at last."

Now I'm home again, after walking in their footsteps. Sometimes I'll be the host, sometimes the guest, sometimes the stranger. And no, I was not busy when you showed up. I do not need to pretend I have a purpose in the world. You are my purpose.

# July Encounter

*by Bob Kee*

It was a July day in 2015, and we were in the Tumacacori mountains to hike a trail that had been active recently. We parked our vehicle at a spot where we could look south and view the trail we had planned to hike. We had parked or stopped here numerous times over the years, but never did we see anyone. This particular day was different, and we did spot an individual walking north approaching a Green Valley Samaritan water and food drop.

We put on our backpacks and walked down to meet the gentleman. He was surprised to see us so we immediately identified ourselves as Tucson Samaritans. We told him of our mission and the reason for us to be in the desert. He was a man in his 40's from Altar, Mexico and he told us his name was Manuel. He said he had a kiosk in Altar, Mexico, and sold supplies to migrants, but the traffic had slowed so he and a few friends decided to travel north in an effort to find work. He did not go into detail but told us he had been separated from his friends. We explained to him that it was not possible to walk with us. That would look like we were aiding his movement north and that was against the law. He understood and waited 10 minutes or so before proceeding behind us.

We would stop periodically for breaks due to the heat and terrain. Manuel would catch up so we would have time to chat before we ventured on again with him traveling a quarter mile or so behind.. After walking about 3 1/2 miles, we realized it was time to turn around and head back to the vehicle as we could see the clouds starting to build up in the south. At our last stop we wished him well, and he continued on as we retreated to the safety of our vehicle.

We continued back on the same trail when about 3/4 of a mile from our vehicle, we encountered another gentleman on the trail. It appeared he was out for a stroll with nothing but a liter bottle that was only half full of water. We stopped to talk and let him know who we were and that we could help him with food and water. He also identified himself as Manuel and told us the same story as our first Manuel encounter. A young woman in our group offered up her backpack for him and as we were filling it with food packets and bottles of water, Manuel suddenly said, "stop" because he felt someone else might need the supplies. We assured him that we were close to our vehicle which contained more supplies should we have another encounter. He finally accepted our offer, then continued on his journey north.

We wished him well as he left, and stood there, quite stunned and momentarily speechless. Here was someone that literally had almost nothing on this hot July afternoon, and his thoughts were immediately of others.

I still remember thinking that this man is a better man than I, because I believe my thoughts at that moment would have been solely about myself and my survival. I also remember thinking that I would love to have this man as a friend and neighbor. Many years later, those memories are still quite vivid.

# The Unseen Clothing Ladies

*by Val Chiong*

I have had the time, on occasion, to help the "Clothing Ladies" who manage a warehouse-size room loaded with donations for migrants at the United Methodist Church basement in Tucson. It is a virtual department store of items no longer needed by their owners: Toiletries, toys, shoes, backpacks, diapers - you name it - it is down there. It is an overwhelming task that is ongoing and empties and fills at a rapid pace. There are bags and boxes as far as you can see.

But let me tell you, these ladies have a plan. Sort, wash, mend, iron, repair, match and size - these ladies are professionals. Such care and love in every step. They chat and prepare matching sets of clothes for the kids and adults alike. They laugh and sort away the hours in that basement and all without recognition or the chance to witness the joy and dignity they give to those who are now wearing their washed, mended, ironed, sorted and distributed clothing.

# Ouma

*by SuEllen Shaw*

## A Gift From the Heart

The lunch room at the Drexel Center holds ninety-eight men from all over the world: men seeking asylum, legally here, delivered by ICE or the BP. Some have been on the road or in camps at the Border for months. The dining room is full. Then a young mother and her 4-year old child, who are sheltered in another area, enter. Mother waits by the door for a baby bottle that a volunteer prepares. As she waits, eyes turn in her direction. But they do not see her. All eyes dwell on the black haired, shy child holding onto his mother's leg. The men smile and light up, thinking perhaps of home and their own children or family left behind? Perhaps delighting in both the innocence and the hope a young child presents? Then, a young, smiling Mauritanian man gets up and walks to the child; he cannot resist. He hands the little boy his apple, reaches his right hand to shake hands, and says his name. With Mama's prompting, the boy shakes hands, smiles shyly and says, "Tomas. Gracias." The whole room heaves a sigh and smiles as the child slowly bites into the red apple.

## Ouma

"Thank you, Ouma." "Thank you, Ouma." I had to look it up: "from South Africa, grandmother or title of respect for any older woman." These Black African men, thanking me for the water I pour in their glasses at the Drexel lunch room, have given me, despite their struggles for safety and asylum, a gift: they have shared something of their home life and language with me, the respectful honorific for the elder women in their lives. We have no such term of respect in our country. "Grandmother" is usually limited to those blood relatives in that position. This gift, though small, is more than enough to make me smile and wish them well.

## Never Letting Go

A young woman with her two young children, aged about 5 and 7, struggles off the bus driven from the Nogales Border, and hesitantly enters the building. Backpacks and other travel bags weigh her down as she shepherds her children forward. Her downcast eyes and face emit exhaustion and despair. But then, she hears a shout. She looks up. A young man, who arrived hours earlier and has been desperately watching arrivals, runs toward her from his chair in the back of the courtyard, the holding area of Casa Alitas. He calls her name: "Maria!" Her look of despair turns to relief and joy. The man engulfs her in his embrace. The tiny children cling to his legs. They all stand and weep until finally, never letting go of one another, they move as one to the chairs where he wraps them all in his blanket. They have been separated for too long.

## Woman to Woman

I walk into the women's restroom and am stopped immediately. A woman, crying softly, stands by the Tampax dispenser. It takes quarters. The woman reaches out, hands me a dollar bill and points at the machine, frantic questioning on her face. She has no quarters. I carry no money to the welcome center and briefly wonder again, why even at Casa Alitas, where desperation abounds, women must pay for obvious necessities. I motion her to wait. I return to the dining room to ask the other lunch servers if any have quarters, explaining the woman's dilemma. No one has money of any kind. I go to the office and am told to check at the clothes bank. Fortunately, it is open. The volunteer there has no tampax, but she does have a large aluminum bowl full of individually packaged pads. Grabbing a handful, I return to the restroom. As I hand the pads to the tearful woman, she smiles and, hand on her heart, heaves a sigh of relief. I wonder about the rationale for keeping the bowl hidden away in the back of a huge clothes room filled largely with men's clothes.

## Needing to Work

Today there are three of us lunch volunteers to handle the serving. Sara, our lead, handles the door, checking diners in and doing the hand sanitizing. Betsy hands the plates of pizza to the diners as she invites them to take a water glass and an apple and then moves around, trying to answer questions or converse. I am arranging and loading plates of cheese pizza from the 65 pizza boxes delivered by Pizza Patrol. The pizzas are cut into 8 slices each for distribution of two pieces to a plate. The line is long, about 200 men. They are hungry, but patient. I have started filling plates before the doors open, but I am falling behind as I struggle to stay ahead of the line. Suddenly, a young man steps out and comes up beside me at the counter. He starts pulling the paper plates apart and arranging them on the counter for me to fill, handling one part of my job for me. As each box empties, he closes it and stacks it for me with the other empties against the wall. He continues to help until the line has finished. I learn he is from Mauritania on the west coast of Africa. He is more comfortable speaking French than English, so he does much of his communicating in sign language. I have also learned he is very good at seeing how to help. As diners finish, he delays eating his well-earned pizza and starts wiping tables. His welcome help is typical. Most guests bus their own tables and wipe them down. Many open doors, move furniture, fill water igloos, offer to sweep or remove trash, or serve as interpreters when we volunteers don't understand our guests' attempts to talk with us. Their willingness to help demonstrates both their need to give back and their desire to work and do something useful. Unfortunately, the laws in our country do not make working here easy. While they are here legally, they wait at least six months and often longer for work visas that cost from 480 to more than 1,000 dollars, depending on their status and application. Meanwhile, they must also plan for their asylum hearings. They must pay not only the attorney's fees, but also other costs associated with preparing an asylum case, such as a psychological evaluation and expert witness services. Yes, they need and want to work, while their families at home await their support.

# The Salad Maker

*by Connie Aglione*

We spotted the young man with his back-pack standing under a tree off the side of a rutted road and greeted him in our limited Spanish, "Hola. Somos Samaritanos. Necessita ayuda?" He replied in English, "Good Morning. Thank you."

We continued conversing in English and quickly learned that Luis was traveling alone back from Mexico where he had gone to see his grandmother. He was not sick, or weak or injured and didn't need any clothing. But he accepted a couple bottles of water and granola bars and seemed happy for some company. He intended to continue on his journey and was hoping to get to a place soon where he could phone his brother.

"I live in New York", Luis said.

"I'm from New York!" I said

"I work in a restaurant there. Maybe you know it."

I was thinking, "what is the chance, in all of New York, I would know the one restaurant where he works."

"It's the Riviera in the Bronx. They have all the big weddings. I work there with my brother and cousin."

To my amazement I did know it. "Yes! I've been there for two family weddings," I answered, picturing the grand wedding venue by the water.

Luis, smiling, continued, "I'm the salad man. I make all the salads for the dinners." Then he enthusiastically added, "They are starting something new. They have a boat at the dock. People can rent it for engagement parties and showers." I then remembered I had attended a bridal shower at The Riviera too.

Luis and I enjoyed our unlikely connection but knew we soon had to wrap up our little encounter. Luis needed to be on his way and it wasn't safe for us to draw attention to him from anyone who might be driving by, especially Border Patrol. So, we three Samaritans said our goodbyes, me reverting to my elementary Spanish, "Vaya con Dios, Luis." My prayers are with him still.

We've all heard the negative commentary. Who are these migrants? I want to tell everyone: sometimes they are the charming young men preparing salads for your niece's wedding.

# CHAPTER 9
# STRENGTH

# Poetry in Action

*by Chris Affolter*

I've seen them,
Homeless and huddled
Hand holding hand
Hearts filled with hope
Following the footprints
Of my grandfather
Yours too
Under the very same
Stars in the sky
Ending one story
Beginning another
Risking it for the promised land
Painted red white and blue
Sleeves rolled up
Ready to work
Ready to love
They are the brave in
The land of the free.

# Alberto

*by Roger Kleckner*

His finger was red and swollen to the point that the skin was starting to crack. He was a thin man with a thin mustache and sunglasses, wearing a blue baseball cap and blue windbreaker. He held his head high. His name was Alberto.

He had crossed the desert without documents in the dark and had damaged his finger trying to brace for his fall down the side of an arroyo. When the Border Patrol apprehended him, his finger was already badly infected.

After having been dropped off by the U.S. Border Patrol, he started walking back into Mexico and made his way to our humanitarian tent, a place where returning migrants could get food, water, coffee, and other supplies. We examined his finger and told him he needed a doctor. He shook his head no, fearing they would amputate it.

Shura, a Samaritan, did get him to agree to go into Nogales and get some antibiotics at a pharmacy. She talked a Mexican into lending us his car and she asked me if I would drive. I said that I didn't know the way. She said that she did, so I agreed.

The car was dented, rusty and the driver's door was stuck so I had to crawl in from the passenger side. It did start and we were on our way, shaking and rattling. Shura told me to turn left at the next road. As I made the turn, she added, "I think." "You think?!" I shouted. She smiled and we continued. A couple of turns later we were in the city of Nogales at a busy intersection. We didn't know which way to go. A man on the sidewalk somehow figured out from our broken Spanish, hand signals and forlorn looks that we needed to find a place to park.

He waved for us to follow him, and he quickly led us to a yard. We gave him a dollar and walked to a pharmacy. After entering and explaining our situation, the lady said we needed a prescription from a doctor. She then told us that there was a walk-in clinic nearby. Maybe they could help.

At the clinic, the doctor hadn't yet arrived but was expected, so we waited. When he arrived, we were relieved that he spoke English. After explaining who we were and our situation, we followed him into a room and he started to examine the finger and clean out the dirt and sand. The man never said a word, but his face said he was in extreme pain. I was sitting across the table from him, and I offered my hand like we were going to arm wrestle. He grasped my hand and squeezed. He was thin, but very strong. My hand grew numb.

Soon the doctor was finished, and he left us, returning with pills and tubes of antibiotics, likely samples given out by drug-reps. He applied ointment to the finger and wrapped it. Alberto swallowed a couple of pills. In Spanish the doctor explained quite forcefully to Alberto how to use the antibiotics and the ointment. Alberto nodded his head.

We asked what the charge would be. The doctor asked, "Are you charging him for your help?"

We said, "No" and the doctor replied, "Neither will I". The doctor recommended that we should get the man a meal as the pills he had just taken were pretty strong on an empty stomach.

We thanked him and went to a restaurant close by and bought Alberto a hearty meal which he quickly consumed.

Saying good-bye, Alberto walked away after thanking us many times.

We got back to our rust bucket and returned to the tent. Now we knew the way.

When we got back, we learned that we had been gone for so long the owner of the car thought we may have stolen it.

Six months later, I was back in Nogales, Sonora, with a group and we were visiting a church. I stepped outside alone and stood there looking around. I heard behind me, "Senor! Senor!" I thought someone was going to ask me for money but when I turned around, I recognized Alberto. With a big grin he raised his hand. His finger was completely healed. We hugged and after many "gracias" and "de nadas", he walked around the side of the church. I waited a few seconds relishing the moment. I followed him looking up the street and hoping to catch a final glimpse of Alberto. He was nowhere to be seen.

# Wilmer

*by Lynn Nowakowski*

More than ten years ago my husband and I were driving a van loaded with food and clothing for the Comedor in Nogales, Sonora. It was a cold, dreary morning after a night that had reached freezing temperatures. We stopped when we saw a small, young man weaving and stumbling down the median on I-19. He told us his name was Wilmer and both his parents had been killed in a bus accident several years earlier. He and his group of friends, traveling from Honduras, had lost contact with each other during the night when a Border Patrol helicopter had flown directly above them causing them to scatter.

Before the journey, he and his friends had worked on a coffee plantation and slept on a dirt floor while making approximately five dollars for a ten to twelve hour day. Because they were healthy young men, the cartel targeted them to be drug runners. They knew their country wasn't safe for them so they fled.

Wilmer was nineteen and headed to Florida where a distant family member from Honduras offered him work and a place to live. Sitting in our car we feared he was in the beginning stages of hypothermia. We warmed him up, gave him food and made contact with the people in Florida. Within minutes two angry border agents arrived and roughly pulled him out of the van screaming, "Armas-Armas!" (Weapons!) as they dragged him to their truck. He was so scared, cold, hungry and gentle with pleading eyes directed at the agents and us. Luckily we had his family's number in our phone and could keep in touch with each other.

We learned that after being deported and dropped off in the middle of the night on a street in Mexico, the cartel found Wilmer. They searched him and discovered the Florida contact information. They proceeded to extort money four times over a month saying they would kill Wilmer if the family did not comply.

The first demand for money was to simply get him across the border again. The second to pay expenses to take him to Las Vegas. The third for fake identification papers and lastly to drive him to Florida. He was threatened and held at gunpoint in 'safe' houses the entire time. In the end they put him on a bus to Florida with twenty dollars.

We remained in contact with Wilmer and he told us that being in Florida was not what was promised. He made his way to the midwest where he found friends and was hired by a Mexican restaurant. He graduated from high school while working full time and was selected to be a mentor to others who had been through the same experience. The staff and counselors had very high regard for Wilmer. For the past five years he has had his own roofing company and hires others who are trying to make a living and a life in the US. Wilmer is happily married and has two lovely children.

We respect and admire Wilmer and are so fortunate to have met him on the highway that cold morning so many years ago.

# One Lollipop/Paleta

## At a Time

### by Val Chiong

I have been volunteering in the Tucson sector and across the border in Nogales, Mexico with migrants, refugees and asylum seekers for about 6 years. My experiences have changed with the times.

We are no longer allowed to prepare meals and no longer have time to sit and share a meal together. This has changed my experience and that of our guests. Some intimacy and interchange has been diminished, however, the need and appreciation has not. Every smile and thank you is as rewarding as ever.

Even though my Spanish has improved, I still stumble and mumble my way through. I am especially drawn to children from infant to teen, and they never cease to amaze me ; they are able to find joy in the smallest places.

I love to walk through the groups of adults huddling over their phones trying to find the connections they need to move their families and lives forward. I see the children lazing on their parents, tugging on their siblings, crying for attention, looking for comfort. As I approach there is sometimes apprehension or curiosity, "who is this lady and why is she smiling at me? I don't know her." But once I reach into my pocket and withdraw a lollipop, I've got their attention.

"¿Quieres paletas?" I ask in my accented Spanish Now they are interested and give me a big smile, and a very sweet,"gracias"! This simple act reaches them and hopefully restores a bit of trust back into their world.

# Sacrament at the Border

*by Richard Chamberlin*

## Sacrament at the Border

Driving along the 32 feet high border fence
up and down rolling hills
in an ocean of desert
surfing down one then up the other.
suddenly we spot a group of
antlike figures on the horizon
the engine whines in low gear
as we race down a 45-degree slope
then up the next rise
as we get closer someone is waving at us
we reach the top and pull over
a dozen migrants congregate around the jeep
They say they are out of food, water.
Pastor Randy, the driver, asks them how long
they've been there
"Two days waiting for the Border Patrol,"
comes the answer
"Coyotes took all the money we had.
Now we have nothing," said a woman.
We hand out bottles of water, protein bars, chips, cans of tuna
and little fuzzy animals for the kids.
a woman propped against the fence
is crying as a friend comforts her.
she has run out of blood pressure medication
and is afraid she's going to die.
An SUV from *No More Deaths*
pulls up. They have a medic.
I ask her if she has a blood pressure cuff;
she doesn't. Randy climbs to the top of a rise,

calls the Border Patrol,and comes back.
"They said they know they're here."
"What are they waiting for?" I ask.
He shrugs and holds out his hands.
Later we head back on the border road
to our comfortable lives. We pass four other
groups of migrants huddled along the fence
trying to shield themselves from the wind.
We stop and give aid.
Construction equipment lines the road.
Holes in the wall are being repaired.
suddenly we see three green and white Border Patrol SUVs
coming toward us
moving in the direction of the migrants
carrying with them
a sacrament of dust from the desert.

# Two Strangers Meet

*by Melinda Louise*

His hands were dirty,
His jeans were ripped.
His pleas for help at my gate were preceded
By the stench on his clothes and on his skin from his wandering
In the desert.
He had an unrelenting thirst,
And his belly was empty. He was tired, so tired,
And his feet were sore.
He was reaching out to me in sheer desperation.
Despite his fears and despite my own,
What I saw in his eyes and he in mine, was trust.
For me, an opportunity to help a fellow traveler on the highway of life.
For him, a needed respite.
His place of origin, his home, Guatemala.
His destination, his new home, New York City. His journey, a long one.
In his heart burned a desire so strong he could not be deterred.
On faith alone he was, against all odds, on a path to a better life.
His determination and desperation opened my heart and opened my mind,
Bringing me the richness that comes from helping a stranger along the way.
He never knew the blessings he brought: hope, faith, trust.
I think of him often. I hope he arrived safely at his destination.
I hope that along the way he, too, found that same spark of richness
that he had brought to me.
Two strangers, one brief meeting and the world shifts, ever so slightly.

# Living in the Borderlands of Southern Arizona: My Three Take Aways

*by SuEllen Shaw*

## Safety Issues

"Do you feel safe?" Always the same question when family, friends, or others hear where I live. It is not an unreasonable question given the news presented in the media. We hear regularly of drug smuggling, fentanyl busts, human trafficking, property damage and other frightening reports. "Yes, I do feel safe in Southern Arizona." I do not always agree with the tactics of ICE or the Border Patrol. But the agents are a presence at check points on both major highways and in the desert. Their helicopters fly over the desert and the pecan groves near my house, regularly patrolling the Southern Arizona countryside, and at night their strobe lights sweep the arid lands below them.

The Border agents have a heavy job of securing the border and also rescuing the migrants lost or stranded in the desert. The travelers they find are not looking for my neighborhood. Instead they are making their way to Tucson, Phoenix, or other points north. They travel to find work and to reunite with family or friends in cities across the United States. Most illegal drugs now coming into this country are brought across the border in semi trucks or cars not by foot travelers who arrive carrying little but the clothes they wear or children in their arms. So, do I feel safe? Yes.

## Contrasts With Home

I grew up on a wheat farm on the plains of North Dakota. The landscape, terrain, and the wildlife there are as different from Southern Arizona as one might imagine. So living here has been a rich education in plants and animals: learning the varied cacti, agave, and other desert plants; watching the busy geckos and lizards; being fascinated by the javelinas, coatimundis, and coyotes; and learning to recognize all the new birds. The landscape also provides great variety for hiking, walking, biking or driving the trails in Madera Canyon and the Santa Rita or Catalina Mountains.

The cultural diversity and history of the area are very different from the Dakotas. I can listen to a mariachi band from Tucson or Nogales, Sonora, one day and the traditional Green Valley Stage Band the next. While North Dakota certainly has concert bands, a Norwegian or Polish Polka band is much more present than Mariachi. I also have access to the wide variety of ethnic restaurants that make Tucson a UNESCO world heritage site for its cuisine. I have the challenges and pleasure of hearing and learning words of other languages, particularly Spanish. I hear the stories of Father Kino and the Anza Trail, imagine the movement of the Jesuits north from Mexico, and envision early settlements when I visit the Tumacacori and San Xaviar Missions or see DeGrazia's depictions of such in the Gallery of the Sun.

## Meeting the People

Within the natural landscape, between the city of Tucson and the Santa Rita Mountains, lies Green Valley, a retirement community of about 35,000 people during the winter months. Green Valley is just 40 miles north of the US/Mexico border. That means ample opportunity to visit Mexico, just as I visited Canada when I lived 60 miles south of the U.S./Canadian Border. I have enjoyed sight-seeing visits to the San Ignacio Mission and Magdalena in Sonora. I have vacationed at Puerto Peñasco on the Sea of Cortez. Trips like these enable personal contact and informal relations with the residents there. Many of my friends also get that contact when they go to the dentists in Mexico and have lunch there afterwards, something my parents did for many years. The trips have given me a picture that is much more balanced than the narrow view of crime and danger in Mexico that is presented by the U.S. media.

The media also gives a skewed image of the immigrants coming to this country. In past years, I trained to help DACA applicants assemble their documents to stay in this country. I have also volunteered at Casa Alitas, a welcoming center and shelter in Tucson, Arizona, for guests legally in this country awaiting their asylum hearings.

At the center, the travelers are connected to their sponsors, assisted with transportation needs, given food, clothing, and medical treatment if necessary. People from all over the world, not just Central and South America, arrive daily at Casa Alitas, vetted by the U.S. Border Patrol or Immigration and Customs Enforcement (ICE). I help serve lunches there. I am always impressed by the gratitude, politeness, good humor, willingness to help, generosity and respect demonstrated by guests, even after all they have endured in coming to the United States.

My impression is that they are eager to work and give back for what they are receiving. In serving at Casa Alitas and earlier with DACA recipients, I have heard personal stories, seen the smiles and the tears, learned the costs of legal entry and paths to citizenship that I would not have otherwise learned living in the north country.

While some challenges may exist for me living in Southern Arizona, these challenges have been avenues for growth on my part. I understand the work of the Border Patrol more; I have learned to hike in mountain terrain and to recognize [and spell] javelina as well as coatimundi; and I have had opportunities to meet many warm, caring people in my serving at Casa Alitas.

# EPILOGUE

*Mural in the courtyard of The Good Shepherd United Church of Christ, painted collaboratively by participants at Common Ground on the Border, January 2024.*

# The World At Our Border

## John 6:32-35
## Message October 6, 2024

*Randy Mayer*

As a kid growing up in Montana, I thought World Communion was a pretty big stretch of the imagination. I mean, my world was very small. Montana is pretty isolated in its own little world. I just couldn't imagine people speaking in different languages, living in vastly different cultures, eating completely different foods, and living very different lives. There was just no way that I could appreciate that there were nearly five times more Indians living in India at the time than people living in the United States or that Africa is so large that you can put the United States, India, China, and most of Europe into its boundaries and you would still have room for a few more countries. Africa is absolutely enormous! A kid living in a small town in Montana just couldn't begin to ever understand that.

The Montana-NorthWyoming Conference of the United Church of Christ must have recognized my ignorance for when I turned twenty they nominated me to be on the United Church Board for World Ministries. Talk about a fish out of water! I was sitting in large conference centers with missionaries from around the world talking about their work, their culture, and the ways in which the church was making a difference in so many places around the world. I just sat in awe: fascinated and mesmerized. But I was also feeling very out of place and intimidated. Why was I sitting there? I had no worldly experience; I could barely locate countries on the map. I remember saying to myself, "You are a country bumpkin. You have a lot to learn." I needed to stretch my wings and explore the world. For the last 40 years or so I have tried hard to expand my world view, learn a language or two, travel, learn about cultures and ideas, and meet as many people from as many places as possible. Some might even say that I have taken it to extremes by making weekly trips to Mexico, hosting international guests, and traveling far and wide. In the process the world has become a playground that continues to draw me in and transform my ways of thinking.

I am thankful for this experience and the journey I have been on over these years. In fact, we as a church have been on this journey together to broaden our horizons. I am glad we started it a long time ago and have some experience under our belts, especially concerning our work along the border, because the world is literally coming apart at its seams. Desperate people from all over the world who are being threatened with violence, war, climate change and generational poverty are being dumped right at our doorstep. The current situation along the border makes author Gloria Anzaldua's quote come alive: "The U.S-Mexican border *es una herida abierta* (an open wound) where the Third World grates against the First and bleeds. And before a scab forms, it hemorrhages again."

To demonstrate this open wound of the world that is bleeding even today, I have collected a bunch of passports, birth certificates and other ID's or papers that I have found along the border just in the last couple of weeks. You may not know that it is literally the United Nations down there: a modern-day Ellis Island filled with people from all over the world. Here is an Indian passport for Jasvidne or a couple passports from the People's Republic of Bangladesh for Sirajul and Mehedi. Or this copy of a Ghanan passport for Aboul-Wadudu. Or this passport with the photo page torn out from Nepal. I have this voting card from Alfredo from San Cristobal de las Casas, Chiapas, Mexico and this Birth Certificate from Noe from Ocosingo, Chiapas—born on October 26, 2010. Soon he will be 14 years old. Here is a receipt from the Fiscal General of Ecuador, a phone card from Egypt, and a plane ticket from Amsterdam to Sao Paulo, Brazil. Who would have thought? All of this just a few miles from us right here. We are in the center of a massive world crisis.

It makes me want to play detective. Who are these people? Why did they leave their homes? Did they leave loved ones behind and will loved ones be here to receive them? I don't have any answers. I just know that people leave for a reason and our world isn't the world that God created it to be. We as a world community have failed. We as followers of Jesus haven't lived into Jesus' great prayer that they may all be one. We have stumbled and fallen in our attempt to follow the ways of Jesus.

Did you know that World Communion Sunday took hold in the aftermath of the Second World War? The world had come to the brink of total destruction. Europe and Japan were in ruins and the human race was stunned by its capacity for violence and destruction: London, Dresden, Coventry, Berlin, Hiroshima, Nagasaki, Auschwitz, Buchenwald. It was a sad sight of what human beings can do to each other. The Protestant churches had a strong presence in all those cities and nations that had suffered so much. The largest concentration of Japanese Christians, for example, lived in Nagasaki and perished on August 9, 1945. Christians obliterating other Christians and non-Christians alike; it was ferocious and barbaric. Christians from around the world tried to find a way to speak a prophetic and healing word that would affirm the oneness of the human race, the precious gift of every human life, and also a word that might translate religious beliefs into work for peace. The idea they came up with was not a political action movement but a day on which the world's Christians would acknowledge and celebrate their oneness at the Lord's Table. And so on the first Sunday of October, Christians all around the world join hands across barriers of race and nationality.

The idea of World Communion seems pretty trite. It is going to take a lot more than breaking bread and sitting at the same table for this world to come to its senses, to change its ways, to learn how to respect and honor each other, and to share and lift the other up rather than tear them down. But it is a start.

I don't think it was any different for Jesus in his time. The Roman Empire was brutal, absolutely squashing out any opposition, forcing people to pay taxes and homage to the emperor while they were desperate for even crumbs from the table. Speak out, get out of line, object and you were destroyed, hung on a cross, an example for all to see. Jesus detested it, spoke out against it, and taught a different way: a way of love, and hospitality.

Our passage this morning catches Jesus being chased by the crowds. They are hungry; they want more food for their children. Why not? They are starving to death. Wouldn't you want food too? And Jesus says to them, "I am the bread of life. Whoever comes to me will never be hungry, and whoever believes in me will never be thirsty." It is just as hard for us today to understand this passage as it was two thousand years ago. We too want things immediately. We want the answers and we want the basics. Just give us the directions to get there and we will be there. But the ways of Jesus are much slower; they take time, practice and study to live into and develop.

The early Christians had learned the hard lessons the hard way: They had seen Jesus killed and they had vivid memories of his teachings and his focus on living The Way. In fact they were called People of the Way for they practiced radical love of neighbor, radical hospitality and radical sharing of their resources. They focused on what Jesus taught in this passage about something deeper in life and the practices of faith and community. They remembered the Sermon on the Mount where not one word was about what to believe but everything was about what to do. It was a behavioral manifesto, not a propositional one. But over time things got twisted, people got lazy, and they lost Jesus' focus. It was easier to be in your head spouting off your beliefs rather than actually getting your hands dirty and doing the hard work. They forgot that Jesus was all about the way of life. And three centuries later, when the Nicene Creed became the official oath of Christendom, there was not a single word in it about what to do nor how a Christian should act in the world. The only words left were about right belief! (Adapted from Robin Meyers)

That is why it is so confusing in our world today; popular Christianity has become all about slogans, about praying to God and expecting God to give what you asked for. It has become a destination religion that is all about getting to heaven while completely ignoring the journey. It has become self-centered and all about my, me, mine: my salvation, my protection, watching over my family, my belongings and making me prosperous and wealthy. There is absolutely nothing about walking together, sharing with the community so that all may thrive, radically caring for the neighbor, or putting yourself on the line for the other. When Jesus talked about the bread of life, this is what he was talking about: I am the bread of life, my ways are the bread of life, go and practice them. Believe in my ways and you will never be hungry. Embody them like I have embodied them and you will never be thirsty.

When we practice Jesus' ways, little by little our rough edges are worn smooth and our minds are slowly transformed from a focus on fear and survival to a focus of compassion and radical love. Our violent and vindictive ways become focused on peace and offering hope. We stop waging war and start washing feet.

The end of the border wall, that *herida abierta*, the open wound where all those personal documents and passports are recovered, has been proclaimed dangerous by the media and politicians on both sides: a no man's land where all the criminals, rapists and delinquents gather. I have been going out there for nearly 25 years and I have never feared for my life. We have created a camp, a shelter from the storm out at the end of the wall, where vulnerable people can gather in safety as they legally wait for the Border Patrol to come and take them to the station where they can make their case for asylum.

This camp has become a place of radical compassion and care: Just this last week I talked to three men from Nepal who had been on the road for 9 months while also carrying the back pack of an elderly man from

Colombia; a single woman from Ecuador that had traveled for 2 and ½ months all by herself emotionally supported by women from Guerrero, Mexico; and 3 unaccompanied minors (ages 8, 10, and 15) from Chiapas, Guatemala, and Honduras who became friends along the way and take care of each other.

In this camp something miraculous takes place. A man from Ghana sees three exhausted mothers sitting with a daze in their eyes from the traumatic journey. He picks up some fruit to offer to them. A man from Argentina goes around and picks up trash. Three men from India have carried bags of special food from their homeland. Just before the Border Patrol loads them in their vehicles, they offer us an unopened bag of Spicy Potato Noodles as an offering of gratitude.

It reminds me of the words from national best-selling author Rachel Held Evans, a young fundamentalist Christian who died way too early. She took her faith journey seriously and slowly smoothed her rough edges and became a bridge between the evangelical and progressive wings of the church. She wrote: "But the gospel doesn't need a coalition devoted to keeping the wrong people out. It needs a family of sinners, saved by grace, committed to tearing down the walls, throwing open the doors, and shouting, "Welcome! There's bread and wine. Come eat with us and talk." This isn't a kingdom for the worthy; it's a kingdom for the hungry."

I believe in that Kindom of God. I believe that is more in keeping with Jesus' vision of the world and the movement he was creating. And on this World Communion Sunday, I think the world would be a much better place if we would make that our focus; simply follow Jesus' way, letting him be the bread of life in our lives.

For in the end, the Kindom of God is like a bunch of outcasts and oddballs gathered at a table; not because they are rich or worthy or good, but because they are hungry; because they said yes. And there's always room for more. Amen

## Invitation to Communion

Each time we come to this table, we recognize Jesus' teaching about the Realm of God not only in words, but with signs and symbols.

Especially on this World Communion Sunday, we recognize the table does extend globally, from our doorsteps to the ends of the earth. From Yugoslavia to Yuma, from Austria to Zambia, from Zanzibar to Shanghai!

All are welcome! Whether we share our traditional elements or breads we brought to celebrate with our siblings around the world, whether the cup is filled with Welch's Grape or milk and honey, these gifts are for the people of God, gathered in this sanctuary and online.

Symbols like these are for the people of God gathered in house churches, in magnificent cathedrals, in simple sanctuaries and in thousands of homes connected by the internet.

These tiny gifts whet our appetite for the great gathering of God's beloveds from across time and space.

May this feast help energize all followers of Jesus the Christ to live our faith. May God's Spirit inspire us, each, and all, to search for ways we can manifest God's love made visible here and to the ends of the earth.

## Words of Institution

Today, Christ-followers meet in public worship and secret gatherings to break bread together.

Today, in wealthy churches and hovels of poverty, wine is shared. In many different languages, by ordained clergy and volunteer pastors, these words of institution are given:

On the night he was betrayed, our Lord, Jesus, gathered for supper with twelve of his closest friends, his disciples.

He took the unleavened bread of the Passover feast, and when he had given thanks to God for it,

he broke it and gave it to his disciples, saying,
"This is my body, broken for you. Do this in remembrance of me."
In the same way after supper Jesus took the cup and gave it to His
disciples, saying,
"This cup is the new covenant – a new relationship with God,
marked by the forgiveness of your sins. Drink of it, all of you."
And so today, every time we eat this bread and drink this cup,
we remember our Lord's death, and we hope for the day when he
shall come again.
These are the gifts of God for all the people of God.

## Breaking of the bread

We give thanks for this bread,
fruit of the earth and hard work,
a gift of the grace of God.
We break it and share it,
remembering the words and actions,
gestures and glances,
silences and self-offered life
of the teacher from Nazareth.
(Bread is broken and shared)
And we give thanks for the fruit of the vine,
for the joy of communion,
for alliances that endure
in the search for justice and wholeness.
We take the cup,
knowing we are part of a community-people
renewing its covenant with life.
(The cup is filled and shared)

## Prayer after Communion

You have met us at the table, Lord Jesus,

to unite us with you and with brothers and sisters around the world.

Go with us now into that world,

that we might be a living sign of welcome among refugees,

of freedom among the oppressed,

of hope amid persecution,

of peace amid violence,

of living faith amid a culture of skepticism,

and of loving kindness toward the earth and all her inhabitants.

We pray in the name of Jesus, even as we pray that prayer that he taught

us: "Our Father ...".

# Rev. Dr. Randy J. Mayer

Deeply influenced by his time studying and living in Latin America, Randy and his family moved to the Borderlands in 1998 so he could serve as Senior Minister of The Good Shepherd United Church of Christ in Sahuarita, Arizona—35 miles from the US/Mexico border. As immigration and border issues became more and more intense, Randy helped create the Green Valley/Sahuarita Samaritans, a border humanitarian group founded in 2005. Today they have over 150 volunteers and five vehicles that drive the backroads giving food, water and medical care to migrants in the desert---for no one should be dying in our deserts. Randy has been a passionate advocate for border communities and immigrant rights, speaking at universities, seminaries and churches.

# GLOSSARY

**Ambos Nogales** – Both Nogales cities: Nogales, Arizona and Nogales, Sonora, Mexico

**Anza Trail** – refers to the Juan Bautista de Anza Trail from Sinaloa, Mexico to San Francisco, California; established in 1775-76

**Arroyo** - Spanish word for a steep-sided gully formed by the action of fast-flowing water in an arid or semi-arid region, found chiefly in the southwestern United States

**Asylum Seeker** – a person who seeks international protection from danger in their home country; usually already in the United States or waiting to present their case at a Port of Entry

**Baño** – Spanish word for toilet

**Basura** – Spanish word for rubbish, trash, garbage; also sometimes refers to migrant belongings left behind in the desert

**Bienvenido** – Spanish word for welcome

**BORSTAR** – Border Patrol Search, Trauma, and Rescue unit

**Buenos dias** – Spanish greeting for good day

**Border Community Alliance (BCA)** – a nonprofit organization dedicated to bridging the border and fostering community through education, collaboration and cultural exchange

**Border Patrol/BP** – U.S. Customs and Border Protection

**BorderLinks** – a community-based organization where people collectively learn, teach, reflect, share resources, and organize for justice in the borderlands

**BP/ Border Patrol Checkpoint** – a location on or near an international border where travelers or goods are inspected and allowed (or denied) entry

**Bracero Program** – an agreement between the U.S. and Mexican governments that permitted Mexican citizens to take temporary agricultural work in the United States (1942-64)

**Casa Alitas** – a shelter in Tucson offering necessities and travel assistance to asylum seeking families

**Casa de huespedes** – Spanish word for a guesthouse

**Casa de la Misericordia** – a shelter located in Nogales, Sonora which assists and houses migrant families while they wait for their asylum appointments

**CBP** – U.S. Customs and Border Protection

**Comedor** – Spanish word for dining room; also an aid center for migrants in Nogales offering food and respite

**Comida** – Spanish word for food

**Common Ground on the Border** – an annual celebration of the U.S./ Mexico borderlands people and culture hosted by The Good Shepherd United Church of Christ. This gathering is an affiliate of **Common Ground on the Hill** /see below

**Common Ground on the Hill** - in Westminster, Maryland, whose mission is: "to encourage and facilitate dialogue, by way of the arts among different cultural traditions, in order to discover that this artistic common ground unites us, and that, as a result, the world might become a more humane place." commongroundonthehill.org

**Coyote** – Spanish word for a person who smuggles immigrants across the U.S./Mexico border; also the name of a wild dog

**DACA**–Deferred Action for Childhood Arrivals, a program begun in 2012 to provide temporary protection from deportation for certain migrants

**Darién Gap** - a remote and treacherous area on the border between Columbia and Panama, dangerous to travel because of the harsh geography as well as the traffickers and robbers who prey on migrants.

**De nada** – Spanish for you're welcome

**Deportee** – a person who has been or is being expelled from a country for violation of immigration laws

**Desconocido** – Spanish for unknown; los desconocidos refers to the unknown, unnamed migrants who have died in the desert

**Desert search** – Samaritans search back roads and trails looking for migrants in distress.

**DHS** – U.S. Department of Homeland Security; oversees BP, CBP, and ICE

**Drexel Center** –a respite center in south Tucson, AZ that offered assistance to migrants (no longer operating)

**El Comedor** – an aid center for migrants in Nogales, Sonora, Mexico that provides two meals a day to migrant men, women and children at all stages of their journeys; some are deportees, and many are seeking asylum.

**Eloy**– town in Arizona with two detention centers operated by the private company Core Civic.

**EMT** – Emergency Medical Technician, and EMTs are medical professionals who provide emergency care and transport patients to medical facilities.

**Father Kino** – an Italian Jesuit missionary and explorer in what is today Sonora, Mexico and southern Arizona (1645-1711)

**Florence** – town in Arizona with two immigrant detention centers; one has an immigration court on-site and is operated by the private company Core Civic; the other is owned by the Federal Government but staffed by a private security company.

**The Good Shepherd United Church of Christ** –a mainline Protestant church known for its progressive theology and emphasis on social justice

**Green Valley** – a retirement community in southern Arizona, 40 miles from the U.S./Mexico border

**Gracias** – Spanish word for thank you

**Halal** -Halal is an Arabic term meaning "permissible" or "lawful" in Islam; when referring to food it means food and drinks that comply with Islamic dietary laws

**Herida abierta** – Spanish word for open wound

**Hija** – Spanish word for daughter

**Humane Borders** – a non-profit and non-partisan organization in south Tucson that operates dozens of permitted water stations in the Sonoran Desert along the Arizona/Mexico border wall and routes used by migrants

**Humanitarian Parole** – individuals who are outside of the United States may be able to request parole (conditional entry) into the United States based on urgent humanitarian reasons or a significant public benefit

**ICE** – U.S. Immigration and Customs Enforcement

**Immigrant** – a person who moves from their country of birth to another, usually seeking a permanent change

**La Migra** – informal Mexican and American Spanish language term for U.S. Immigration & Customs Enforcement, U.S. Border Patrol, and related institutions

**Migrant** – a person who moves from place to place, within a country or, in common usage, between countries

**Mochila** – Spanish word for backpack

**No More Deaths** – a non-profit, humanitarian organization based in southern Arizona functioning as a ministry under their fiscal sponsor, the Unitarian Universalist Church of Tucson

**Perdido** - Spanish word for lost

**POE** – Ports of Entry are places where people can lawfully enter the country, usually along the border, and at airports and seaports.

**Pollo** – Spanish word for chicken; used by people smugglers to refer to migrants

**Quinceañera** – Spanish word for family birthday celebration of a 15-year-old daughter

**Refugee** – a person outside of their native country who is unwilling or unable to return because of persecution or a well-founded fear of persecution due to a variety of factors

**RHR** – recovered human remains

**Samaritans** – founded in 2005; The Green Valley/Sahuarita Samaritans provide water, food, first aid, and other essential items to migrants who cross the border in southern Arizona.

**Saguaro** - an iconic cactus found only in the Sonoran desert and culturally significant to the Tohono O'odham Nation whose people have called this land home for thousands of years

**Sonoran Desert** - a hot desert and ecoregion in North America that covers northwestern Mexico as well as part of the Southwestern United States (in Arizona and California). Hundreds of miles of the US-Mexican border go through the Sonoran desert.

**Tohono O'odham land** - lands of the Tohono O'odham Nation in the Sonoran Desert, a vast area of mountains and valleys, approximately the size of the state of Connecticut

**Vaya con dios** – Spanish phrase for go with God

**Viande** - French for meat

**Wash** - a dry riverbed or creek that temporarily carries water during heavy rains.

**Water drop** – Green Valley/Sahuarita Samaritans leave clean water at multiple sites along migrant trails; sites are checked and re-stocked twice a week.

**Water igloos** – large, usually 10-gallon, coolers for water or other beverages

# WORKS CITED

Anzaldúa, Gloria, *"Borderlands/La Frontera - The New Mestiza,"* San Francisco: Aunt Lute Books,1987.

Evans, Rachel Held, *"Searching for Sunday: Loving, Leaving, and Finding the Church,"* Nashville: Thomas Nelson Inc, 2015, p.149.

Meyers, Robin R., *"Saving Jesus from the Church: How to Stop Worshiping Christ and Start Following Jesus,"* New York: Harper Collins, 2009, p.14.

Mortenson, Greg, *"Three Cups of Tea,"* Penguin Books, 2007.

Nye, Naomi Shihab, "Red Brocade" from *The Tiny Journalist: Poems,* Rochester: BOA Editions Ltd, 2019.

WORKS CITED

# ACKNOWLEDGEMENTS

Thanks to:

Our writers, members of the Green Valley/Sahuarita Samaritans and members and friends of the Good Shepherd U.C.C., for your tireless support of the migrants. A special thanks for turning your memories into stories and giving your permission for them to be shared with the wider community in this book.

Melissa Lock and Laura Kleckner, our young technical mentors who helped us navigate rough waters and grow more comfortable with the technology needed to turn these stories into a published book.

Dennis and Carol St. John for their help gathering and compiling the stories.

Carol St. John for facilitating border-stories writing workshops that inspired and supported several contributors to this book.

Our photographers Michael Day, Tom Woltjer, Connie Aglione, Kathy Babcock, Randy Mayer, Marge Kinkaid, and Dennis St. John. Their photos helped bring our book to life.

Thanks also to Eric O. Ledermann for the use of his photograph of The Migrant Walk.

© 2015 Eric O. Ledermann, Chandler, Arizona. All rights reserved. Used by permission

Marie Gery for permission to publish her poem, "The Bones of the Teenager." © 2019 Marie Gery

Kathy Babcock for providing a map to help visualize locations mentioned in the book.

With deep gratitude to:

Alma Angelica Macias Mejia (Sister Lika), Director of Casa de la Misericordia, for generously sharing her creative gifts through designing the migrant journey murals, photo images of which appear on the cover and throughout this book.

Randy Mayer, pastor of The Good Shepherd U.C.C. in Sahuarita, Az. Your vision and compassion as a founding member of the Green Valley/Sahuarita Samaritans has truly made a difference in the lives of both the migrants and the volunteers who were inspired to serve. We felt your support every step of the three-year journey from a vague idea to the reality of a published book.

Finally, we honor the migrants who have crossed our paths. Your stories, your presence, and your humanity echo through these pages and remain with us.

# HOW THIS BOOK CAME TO BE

For many years, The Good Shepherd United Church of Christ has opened its doors—and its heart—to sustained reflection on the effects of our broken immigration system on individuals and families. What began as a local gathering has grown into an annual, three-day conference and fair exploring the complex realities of life in the borderlands. Now known as "Common Ground on the Border," the event brings together people from across the country for field trips to border communities, keynote speakers, small-group discussions, and hands-on learning. Music and art weave through the experience, reminding participants that creativity and compassion are essential to understanding one another.

A few days after the 2023 conference, a group of writers gathered in the Spark Arts Studio at The Good Shepherd UCC. Most had just taken part in the conference; several were longtime humanitarian volunteers. What was meant to be an ordinary writing session slowly transformed into something else. Before anyone put a word on the page, we found ourselves debriefing—sharing stories, impressions, and the lingering emotions that had surfaced.

The energy in the room shifted. Compassion quickly became passion—a shared conviction that these stories mattered and needed to be gathered. With support from the pastor—who himself had years of stories to relate—we formed a working group. We clarified our purpose, identified a long list of humanitarians within the congregation, created a process, and reached out across The Good Shepherd community and local Samaritan group. It had become a project.

*The Editors*

# EDITORS

***Connie Aglione*** worked in healthcare as a nurse and social worker in New York before retiring to southern Arizona in 2005. She soon found both community and renewed purpose at The Good Shepherd United Church of Christ and as a volunteer with the Green Valley/Sahuarita Samaritans.

***Kathy Babcock*** retired from careers in high tech and in teaching. After moving to Green Valley in 2005, Kathy was drawn to The Good Shepherd United Church of Christ and the newly formed Green Valley/Sahuarita Samaritans.

*Ellen Curtis* is an American citizen who lives in Toronto, Canada where she spent nearly 20 years of her career in publishing. She has been a winter visitor to Green Valley for 14 years. Her interest in learning about immigration started when she joined what is now called the Arizona Immigration Alliance, a group whose mandate is to educate and advocate for fair legislation and policies on immigration.

*Gail Frank* is a writer, educator and activist. She is the founder and director of Creative Journeys, an organization that creates a safe haven for writers of all ages to tell their stories. She is a long-time columnist and facilitator of writing workshops. As a member of the Green Valley/Sahuarita Samaritans, she writes stories of the migrant experience for websites and newspapers, trying, always, to put a human face on their suffering.

*Deanna Kleckner* is a retired teacher from Ohio who has spent the last 25 winters in Green Valley, Arizona. During that time, she fell in love with learning Spanish and teaching English to Spanish speakers as well as supporting the efforts of the Green Valley/Sahuarita Samaritans.

*LJ Correll Menzel* loved the sun and desert for many winters before finally making Arizona home in 2019. LJ is a retired educator and gallery owner from Wisconsin. Her chance encounter in the desert in 2014 with an SUV of white-haired Samaritan women opened her eyes to the human desperation here and drew her to The Good Shepherd.

www.ingramcontent.com/pod-product-compliance
Lightning Source LLC
Chambersburg PA
CBHW070803280326
41934CB00012B/3038